WRITING GOD'S
OBITUARY

How a Good Methodist Became a Better Atheist

ANTHONY B. PINN

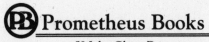

Prometheus Books

59 John Glenn Drive
Amherst, New York 14228

The true mystery of the world is the visible, not the
invisible.

—Oscar Wilde, *The Picture of Dorian Gray* (1891)

I would hurl words into this darkness and wait for an echo,
and if an echo sounded, no matter how faintly, I would send
other words to tell, to march, to fight, to create a sense of
the hunger for life that gnaws in us all.

—Richard Wright, *Black Boy* (1945)

CONTENTS

PREFACE

"Why aren't more African Americans atheists . . . I mean, in light of how Christianity was used to enslave them?"

Over the past twenty years—the time period during which I've done most of my writing and speaking about African American humanists, atheists, and freethinkers—I have heard some version of this question too many times to count. It has peppered Q&A sessions after presentations I've given, and it has followed me down the aisle of many lecture halls.

I don't doubt the question is genuine. But all too often—as I cover my frustration with a smile and a pause before responding—I offer a reply knowing the question is framed by a real lack of knowledge about African American culture and how religion fits into it. And the question often overlooks any recognition of the firestorm that can accompany an African American saying, "Enough of this madness. I don't believe, and I won't sit passively in a church any longer." The famous line from the movie *Network*, "I'm as mad as hell and I'm not going to take it anymore," applied to African American religion, comes with consequences—anything from mockery to isolation on a variety of levels.

Making this proclamation of disbelief gives people pause, but it doesn't mean African Americans haven't taken this step and made pronouncements of their godlessness under their breath. Others have acted out, with a smile covering their anger, this shift away from the church in passive (passive-aggressive) ways. Others, like me, have taken it further and made public statements concerning the irrelevance of theism to the meaning of life.

But to understand this last response, to think about an African American presence in humanist and atheist communities, requires something more than a quick turn to pieces of popular literature by spokespersons of the "New Atheism." You have to know something about us.

Writing God's Obituary is an effort to close this gap by clearing the fog surrounding African American humanism and atheism through the story of how one African American became an atheist. What I have heard and experienced over the years—the quick conversations off to the side, the questions after formal presentations, the e-mails, Facebook posts, and phone calls from other African Americans who find something familiar in my story—grounds my belief that my story says something about more than just me.

My life—the way the church captured me and shaped me, the development of community and relationships read through the archaic demands of the Bible, the overlooking of life for the benefit of some type of spiritual hope for something better beyond this world, the stifling theology that prevents questioning and thinking—contains something of the stories of others.

I hope other atheists reading my story will appreciate my celebration of our way of life and its diversity, and that those not in our community will find in it a way to do what most theists find difficult (and unnecessary): to see and acknowledge atheism's complexity, passions, purpose, and human face.

This book isn't meant to be preachy; it isn't a rabid condemnation of theism. Instead, through my story, with all the gaps and challenges posed by memory, it shows how the very idea of God gets written out of the life of some simply because God and the stuff of belief in God don't function, don't measure up against the compelling demands of life. While not exact, and between the holes in what I can recall, I believe it still tells of how one person stopped trying to be a good Christian at the expense of his integrity, and became a better atheist with his ethics and moral code intact.

I am responsible for the content of this book (and all the photographs are from my personal collection), but I would like to thank my family and friends for their encouragement and support over the years. I must also thank two of my graduate students for their assistance. Biko Gray worked to make certain the photographs were in proper form, and Jessica Davenport prepared the completed manuscript for submission to the publisher, consistent with its style guidelines. Thank you. Finally, I offer my sincere thanks to the staff of Prometheus Books for such careful handling of this project, and for good humor and kind words along the way.

Chapter One

ALWAYS ON DEATH'S DOORSTEP

We don't pick the circumstances surrounding our births. If we did, I might have chosen a different location. Nothing against Buffalo, New York, but it doesn't have the depth or sophistication I find myself drawn to now.

My family lived between Dr. Martin Luther King, Jr. Park and Delaware Park. While Delaware Park was pristine and solidly middle class, King Park was closer to downtown, closer to the "Fruit Belt"—an area of the city, oddly enough, named after fruit but housing some of the most dangerous activities in the city. My stretch of the city, between these two public markers, was working class. But as you moved from King Park toward Delaware Park, the people in the houses in general got lighter in complexion and more solid in their economic position in the city.

It's not that my section of the city was Hollywood-movie bad, but the economic challenges were clear when you looked at it from the suburbs or from the other side of Delaware Park. We always had the basics and more; we were comfortable. My needs were met and most of my wants were addressed. At times we "robbed Peter to pay Paul," as the expression goes, although it would be some time before I knew this was the case.

The highway, just a couple of blocks away from my home, divided the landscape and served as the escape route for those who worked in the city but called the suburbs home.

Image 1. The author as an infant on Christmas Day.

My neighbors were, by and large, blue-collar workers, with some schoolteachers and so on determined to carve out for their families something of the American Dream. We knew each other and felt some responsibility for each other in part because we looked alike. There was the occasional white family in the neighborhood, but for the most part the push to the suburbs left this space for us, with little indication outside the large but almost empty Catholic church nearby there had been a different look to the place some years before my birth.

My parents, the former Anne Hargrave and Raymond Pinn, settled in this neighborhood, not far from their families, and lived in a small house with three bedrooms and one bathroom. My mother; father; two sisters, Joyce and Linda; and brother Raymond (another child, Kenneth, died at the age of five of cancer before my birth) all lived in this house on Florida Street for different stretches of my time in Buffalo. I was there from my birth to my departure for college.

The configuration of people in the house changed as my siblings—at least nine years older than me—moved on and out. But one thing among my family remained consistent: fragile health and compromised physical bodies. My father, for as long as I can remember, struggled with diabetes—complicated by his smoking and drinking—and he would lose both legs before his death in 1999. One of my early memories is of him receiving his insulin shot; I vaguely recall the needle as I sat there on the floor, hoping I wouldn't end up with a needle like that going into me. While the ramifications of my father's diabetes were a bad image for a child, my mother's health had a more profound effect on me.

She'd developed rheumatic fever and heart disease as a teenager, and over time ended up having two open-heart surgeries to replace a damaged heart valve.

My mother had a large scar on her chest, where surgeons had opened her up to get to her heart. I remember that scar—long and smooth, dotted on each side—marking where her chest was opened and sewn back together. That scar became associated with life for me, its fragility, uncertainty, pain, and joy all wrapped up and held together.

Some of my earliest memories are of my mother in the hospital or sick at home in need of some attention, sometimes an ambulance. I don't recall many nights climbing into bed without the thought going through my head that my mother could be dead or in the hospital before morning. So, I was always aware of death, with it being so very close and beyond anyone's ability to control. My mother couldn't guarantee her health, couldn't assure me I wouldn't end up without her, and I was keenly aware of this.

I never felt secure and never felt my parents could do anything with super strength. I imagine most kids live with the illusion during youth that their parents are larger than life and have the ability to defeat any problem, correct any situation, or comfort against childhood angst, but I had no choice but to be different. I didn't labor under the illusion that they could protect me from everything, that they could even protect themselves. I was aware my parents were just humans, with all the weaknesses and uncertainties associated with being just human.

In the back of my mind was a question I didn't ask my parents until I was much older: "Being so sick, why did you have another child?" Because my mother had undergone open-heart surgery and was on a variety of medications, her doctor told her that having another child would be unwise—

downright dangerous for her and the child. My mother and father weren't young at that point, so why take the risk? Weren't four enough? The doctor wasn't certain the condition of her heart would allow her to bring a baby to term, and the various medications could present health complications for a baby. Despite this advice, my parents had me.

My father didn't respond to the question, but we didn't talk much anyway. We spent time together, but we were distant and didn't ever really get along, although until I was roughly ten, he was around and did what he could (and how he could) to be "present" by taking me to piano lessons and Little League games and by watching TV programs with me on the couch and he in his La-Z-Boy chair, cigar or cigarette in his mouth and the ashtray nearby. My mother responded by calling me her "miracle baby."

She'd say, "God has the answer. You were born to be my comfort in my old age. That's what an old woman said when she first saw you as a baby."

Needless to say this perspective on my birth, as the youngest of five children, meant a special bond with my mother and, by extension, with her side of the family.

Like my father's family that had moved from Virginia to Buffalo, New York, as part of the "Great Migration," the Hargraves moved from Halifax, North Carolina.

Both families were responding to the promise of a new day, new opportunities, and better lives because of Bethlehem Steel right outside of Buffalo, in Lackawanna. I never liked visiting Lackawanna, where some of my father's family lived. The houses depressed me; the fake brick siding made me sad, and the whole city seemed covered by a red dust I just knew came from the large and imposing steel plant. I still have a feeling of desperation, of unease—a desire for movement to get away from the red dust—whenever I think about Lackawanna.

My father's family and my mother's family worked to make a life in western New York; this they had in common, but they differed in that my mother's parents—Annie Whitehead Hargrave and Ashley Hargrave—were college educated. She'd served as a teacher in North Carolina, and he'd done what most college-educated black men did during the early twentieth century: he got by doing what he could to earn a living for his family. But in the North this education seemed to make a difference, to give him a different take on what was possible. Ashley Hargrave eventually left manual labor and opened a few dry cleaners in Buffalo, and a good number of their children—thirteen in all—worked for him. The sign of his success was a big house for his family on Northland Avenue, in what was then a predominately white neighborhood.

My father's family was difficult to know, with only a few exceptions, and the long drive to Lackawanna wasn't the full reason for this distance. My paternal grandfather died when I was young, and all I could remember about him was a faint image of a tall, light-skinned, and thin man standing in a doorway in a white shirt, black vest, and black pants. My grandmother wasn't someone we spent a great deal of time with; from what I could gather, she wasn't particularly fond of my mother. One of my father's brothers, Robert, and his wife and kids were the only ones we really ever visited and with whom I spent any time.

Because Northland was only blocks from my home on Florida, we spent a lot of time with my mother's parents. I have memories of being with my grandmother in one of the dry cleaners, the one around the corner from their home. I remember something about being with my grandfather in the other shop, but what I recall most vividly is the time in church with my grandfather.

He was a deacon at a small Baptist church in Lackawanna. The Baptist faith was not an unusual choice for people like my grandparents. After all, the first independent, black-owned and operated churches in the United States were Baptist. Each of these and subsequent congregations were autonomous and free to conduct business as they liked, which made a lot of sense to people who'd spent too many years dependent on the whims of others.

I don't know whether my grandfather and the other members of this particular church—even its leadership—really cared about the details of church doctrine. They cared about some version of salvation and the basic steps to getting it and keeping it, but anything beyond that may have been the sole territory of the pastor. Regardless of the particulars, church attendance had a variety of meanings and purposes, including socialization, community formation, spiritual hygiene, and leadership training, among other things.

My grandfather had influence, and as a result, most of my mother's side of the family went to church with some frequency. Even those who didn't really seem concerned with salvation went through the motions often enough to know their way around a church sanctuary and order of service. And they performed religious commitment well enough to keep my grandfather and grandmother content.

While he could still drive, my grandfather would pick the kids up and take them to church, but by the time I was old enough to remember any of this, he wasn't driving. My mother would take us for Sunday school, and this was followed by a full service with my grandfather sitting with the deacons and the grandchildren doing the best we could to entertain ourselves without catching his eye. You didn't want him to see your antics. All he had to do was look in your direction and squint, and you knew you were in trouble. He'd catch you after church, look at your through those dirty, thick glasses, and tell you about yourself. He'd give that stern look, and you would just want to melt, but of course, it didn't stop antics the next Sunday.

Despite the threat of reprimand from Ashley Hargrave, church was something of a playroom—the hymnals were easily transformed into a game of pick the same page. You'd open the book without looking, and another kid would do the same, with the goal of ending up on the same page. There were always adults praising God to imitate and mimic, and the bathroom run gave time to get away, meet up in the hallway, and clown around for a couple of minutes before heading back to the church pew.

I don't remember my mother being with us during most of those services, but I also can't remember a time when she wasn't deep into the church. She was a born-again Christian eager to serve the Lord, despite a husband with no interest in that church "bullshit."

Before their divorce, he'd stay home or go somewhere else, but never to church. I think my mother saw this as a challenge; she'd try to be so Christlike that he'd be convinced and come to Jesus. Until then, they, in biblical terms, were "unevenly yoked"—she, a Christian bound for heaven, and he, a sinner bound for hell.

This seemed a common situation, if the overwhelming number of married women in the church against the limited number of men was any indication. These women prayed for divine intervention to strengthen their families and, on a more selfish note, to demonstrate God's favor for them by answering their prayer and bringing a sinful husband to Christ. In an odd way, there was also something about the suffering, the trauma prior to the conversion—if it ever happened—that they enjoyed. Like Christ, they were suffering for the welfare of others. They didn't have the physical cross of Christ they sang and shouted about, but they had a symbolic cross—an unrepentant husband—who took them through so many trials and tribulations, including drinking, smoking, adultery, bad language, and so on.

The stories were fairly similar: a husband living a life of sin and the long-suffering wife living out the requirements of the gospel by putting up with the wrongdoing and by attempting to model the best of the Christian faith. It seemed few of them had unsaved husbands who lived a boring life, one who just went to work and came home. But that type of husband wouldn't have made such a compelling story, wouldn't have shown the power of God so evident when the worst of sinners changed their lives.

They'd walk into the church, or so they seemed to hope, arm in arm with the miracle Jesus had given them—a husband saved from sin and a new soul in the population of believers. And the community of the faithful would celebrate the strength and benefits of the spiritual commitment these women had shown.

So much of church culture as I understood it involved the signs and symbols, the language, postures, and ethics of this struggle to share one's faith.

I imagine there were also Christian husbands in churches like mine whose spiritual labors were meant to bring a spouse into the community of Christ, but the gender dynamics within churches would make these stories less frequently highlighted and explored. Women, in the churches I experienced, had something of a copyright on this story of the long-suffering spouse.

The preacher—most typically a man—gave the women in churches like mine some sense that men could be righteous; their husbands need only be like the "man of God." For the Christian men in the church, the preacher served as something of a role model—how they should relate to each other and their families, how they should position themselves with Christ, how they should talk, how they should think, and how they should relate to the nonchurch world. This, of course, was before technology made it so easy to quickly learn about the indiscretions of these ministers.

Slipups, whether explicitly discussed or merely hinted at, pointed to the difficulty even preachers of the gospel had in trying to live beyond most human frailties or even to do a better job with temptations and shortcomings than their congregants. It had to be a hard life for the minister—always on display and monitored. But the rewards for embracing this status as spiritual role model could be substantial, particularly in larger churches: a home paid for by others, a free car, fine clothing, and the constant attention of adoring fans.

It doesn't seem these Christian women ever really considered the possibility that they made it easy to conduct the behavior they found objectionable. This is not to blame them for their misery, but simply to say there might be something about the embrace of suffering that conditions us to expect it. Their saintly stance—their standing as good and wholesome Christians within the church—required ongoing misery. They sang on so many occasions: "No cross, no crown." And they counted their metaphorical battle scars (at times literal scars) as the price of their salvation and the salvation of others. These scars, they reasoned, were nothing when compared to the awards they'd receive in the next life, if not in this one.

Women like my mother seemed to have a difficult time not seeing the world through the necessity of suffering. How could they see things differently when they were confronted by the golden cross on the altar at the front of the sanctuary, the stained glass windows glorifying the story of a suffering Jesus, and countless songs and sermons celebrating misery?

It was clear something about this Christian faith required, and rejoiced in, pain and suffering. This discomfort marked life and mapped out progress toward God, and who could complain about it? After all, according to the sermons and songs, God suffered on a cross. Surely we could endure our particular spiritual and physical aches and pains? Redemptive suffering—the idea that our sufferings advance us, refine us, can be used by God as the means by which to bless us—anchored those of faith in their relationships with each other and the "world."

My mother had something over most of the others. Her sources of suffering were greater, so the possibility for God to do a significant work through and for her was also greater. Not only was her husband a sinner, described as being more interested in the local bar and a cold beer than in his soul, but she also was in poor physical health. My mother knew spiritual suffering because of my father, but she also knew physical suffering unlike most in our church community. Suffering was her life—at home, at work, and within her body.

She was vulnerable to her heart condition and its accompanying ailments, and she was profoundly sensitive to my father's slights, but she met each day with dignity and determination. My mother's strength was not fully visible to those who saw only her physical condition. There were times when I was embarrassed by her sense that righteousness meant willing exposure to mistreatment, but I could never deny the strength involved in this moral and ethical outlook. I respected and loved her dearly.

Image 2. The author's mother outside the family home at 348 Florida Street.

My mother wasn't able to bring my father to the church, but she kept trying. Even after their divorce she remained concerned about his soul and prayed for him regularly. She encouraged me to pray for and evangelize him whenever I visited him. Raymond Pinn was on a good number of prayer lists.

Chapter Two

NUNS AND BOOKS

My mother and my sister Linda joined a nondenominational church near my grandparents on Northland Avenue. The building was stately, an older church, one of those left behind as whites moved out of the neighborhood into the suburbs. It was near what had become an economically challenged area off the main drag of Jefferson Avenue.

People in other areas of the city and in the suburbs feared Jefferson Avenue and what it represented for them: drug deals, prostitution, and other markers of urban decay. But this fear glossed over the good things happening in the 'hood; it blinded them to the hardworking people, the values, and vision of the possibility of a good life that grounded so many within this neighborhood. And they rarely visited the churches where so much of this hope was celebrated and acted out.

There are particularly graphic ways in which African Americans in my neighborhood used theistic faith as a security blanket, a hiding place away from the harshness of the world. It became a way to make sense of what appeared a senseless world. The others who didn't go this far in the faith, but who still wanted community and the cultural connection to "blackness" the church made possible, came to church and tried to deal with the more offensive dimensions of that experience for the sake of the connections they did enjoy.

My family, by and large, was counted in that number of people who signed on and bought into the teachings of the Christian faith. All this, of course, required giving one's life to Christ and the symbolic act of joining the church.

An opportunity to do both presented itself right after the preacher's sermon.

The minister—regardless of how well or poorly he or she (less often the case) "preached the word"—opened the doors of the church, welcomed "home" backsliders, and offered salvation and church membership to those who'd been lost. On occasion one of those lost husbands, for whatever reason, would make his way down the aisle of the church and shake the minister's hand; other times it might be a child of one of those long-suffering women who'd finally made his or her way back to the Christian community after having experimented with the "world." More often than not, it was a guest invited by a member or one who had just wandered in on a given Sunday.

Shortly after my mother and sister joined this church, I walked down the aisle to become a member. I'm not certain of my sister's motivations, although she is now very involved in the Christian faith, as she participates in a church community in her hometown and goes on missionary-medical service trips regularly. For my mother, it was about finding a more welcoming church home, one consistent with her style of worship—a bit energetic—and where her theology could take root. Sister Pinn, as she was called at times, quickly began work in various capacities in the church—serving as a stewardess responsible for the cleanliness of the church, safeguarding items needed for worship, and performing other tasks that resembled those of a housemother. She worked with young people and managed the youth choir (and had a good voice herself). She was at church whenever needed. My mother loved that little congregation and took pride in her roles.

Her parents, who lived right down the street, didn't attend. My grandmother's health kept her in the house for the most part, particularly after she stopped managing the family cleaners a block away. At times I wonder if health issues (bad arthritis that twisted her hands and legs) were a convenient reason for not attending church. Perhaps even if her health had been better, Annie Hargrave might have had little use for the typical activities and attitudes associated with church. This is not to suggest in any way my grandmother wasn't upstanding, moral, and ethical in her dealings—as if church attendance is the best indicator of any of this anyway. I'm simply saying her interest in organized religion wasn't clear to me, although her commitment to healthy and honest relationships with people was evident.

Image 3. The author's grandparents, Ashley and Annie Hargrave.

My grandmother had a claim to the Christian faith as far as I could tell, but I wondered if she really was a Baptist Christian or if she was more along the lines of the Unitarian Universalist–type Christian—or, like Howard Thurman encouraged, a follower of Jesus without all the institutional trappings and traps. She had a Bible and spoke the language of Christian virtues but didn't participate in traditional rituals. Whatever the case, she seemed pleased my mother was so involved. If nothing else, it kept her and my grandfather's minds off what was no doubt a bad marriage that my mother tolerated like a trouper. Her ongoing determination to keep the marriage going showed, regardless of my father, that my mother kept high moral values, and this reflected well on a family concerned with its name and reputation in Buffalo.

"Sis," as her brothers, sisters, and parents called her, was living the faith, striving for holiness, and leaving the rest to God. And she was able to keep up good appearances and maintain her faith in a brighter future because of an old idea she held to with all her might. My mother would say, "The Lord will make a way" and "God doesn't give you more than you can bear."

Modest clothing, no cursing, and every effort to remove even the appearance of evil were part of my mother's daily plan. It was almost as if she was determined to hide herself, to become invisible, to downplay her beauty and vibrant nature. She displayed the attitude of the suffering servant at times, a willingness to help others even at her own expense.

It struck me as a hard life that involved a delicate balance required by a God with contradictory characteristics—demanding blood, yet loving and just to the faithful. But there was another side to this Being: this God of the Bible was hard as hell on unbelievers, with some having no choice to change because they had been turned over to a "reprobate" mind. I wasn't certain at a young age what this reprobate mind meant, but it couldn't be good. It was a predicament that caused Pharaoh and his army to drown in the sea, and I didn't imagine it would be any easier on contemporary reprobates.

But my mother seemed to be on God's good side . . . if you overlooked her health issues, unsaved husband, and far-from-problem-free children.

Nothing about the Christianity of my childhood suggested that being on God's side would mean an easy life. I knew my mother's challenges, and I'd heard the story of Job and his suffering for God's sake too many times. In fact, divine favor could bring a firestorm of trouble that the truly faithful accepted with celebration of God's righteousness done in a ritualized fashion.

There was a preservice service before the official 11:00 worship service. During this time songs were sung and testimonies were offered. "Giving glory and honor to God who is the head of my life . . ." is how the regulars would begin their testimonies, and they always included stories of affliction and trials. Whether the resolution had been given at that point or not, they boldly proclaimed God would "make a way out of no way." I remember being impressed with their testimonies of confidence in God and their relationship to God; these stories made them seem larger than life. This time given to publicly acknowledging God and God's work in the world was dominated by adults who had more life experience, but it wasn't restricted to them. Young people, measured by their own life experiences and challenges, were also free to "say a word" for the Lord during testimonial services. When young people stood to testify, they received a particularly intense response from the adults, who were so pleased that the spiritual training they offered wasn't in vain, that the household of the Lord would continue.

My mother was in the church, my sister was in the church, and I was going to be as well. My father always felt my mother was pushing me. "Damn it, leave the boy alone," he'd say with frustration apparent in his voice and on his face as we headed to yet another service.

Despite his objections, there was something that felt natural about church attendance and participation that I recognized and enjoyed even at a very young age. It was entertaining in a way and certainly offered a warmer and more comforting environment than home and the ongoing conflict between my mother's religion and my father's drinking and "misconduct." Church provided a reprieve.

At that young age, well before my teen years, this reprieve involved doing some listening, but mainly seeing friends, looking through the hymnal, long adventures on the way to the restroom, and taking the occasional nap. The church building with its hidden corners, hallways, and visual distractions was for me as important, if not more so, than the content of the service. I was far too young to be awed by the sermon or the heartfelt selection offered by the choir. It was a period of community, of gathering during which normal time was suspended, daily obligations forgotten, and enjoyment was the rule.

I liked the idea of spending time in the house of a God who loved us and did wonderful things for us—if we were faithful and patient (very patient). Because God loved us, we should love God and each other, and all this was worked out each week during a few hours when we dressed in our best clothes, headed to the church, walked down the red carpet to a well-worn spot on one of the pews, and "fellowshipped," as the older members of the church put it.

The day I joined the church contained these basic elements of church life.

It was a typical Sunday for me, except for the end when I made my way to the altar. I had fallen asleep, but what can you expect from a small child when a worship service can be so very long? My mother says I awoke and asked what people were doing in the front of the church. She remarked that they were joining this church and making it their church home. I told my mother that "I wanted to join the church too," and I made my way to the front of the sanctuary. I gave the secretary my name and had to correct her when she got it wrong: "My name is Anthony Bernard Pinn," I told her. The secretary needed to get it right . . . Anthony Bernard Pinn.

People were pleased that this young person was joining the church—another soul brought into the kingdom, another soldier in the army of the Lord! For my mother it was part of God's plan for me. Members of the church came up after I stated my name. They shook my hand, hugged me, and welcomed me in.

I don't remember finding this a particularly compelling experience. It wasn't traumatic, but it wasn't all that memorable either. After all, there wasn't much for such a young child to be saved from. What important sins could I have committed at that age?

It didn't really matter. I was a sinner simply because I'd been born into original sin, the consequence of humanity's failure to abide by the will of God. At some point, when I could be held accountable for myself, I was going to have to acknowledge and fix this situation by surrendering my life to God: "For God so loved the world that he gave his only begotten son . . ."

Acknowledging this divine arrangement in response to sin extended to joining the community of the like-minded, of the faithful; but at such a young age?

In hindsight, the situation meant thinking up sins for which I could be guilty and turning trivial things—I didn't tell that I ate the cookies or I lied about homework—into signs of a more fundamental depravity. My misdeeds were fairly minor, or so you might think, but still the taint of original sin was ever-present and damning.

I did well in school, looked clean-cut in my demeanor, and was nonthreatening in my conversation, at least away from home. I was like St. Augustine, the early church leader and theologian on this score: he emphasized in his autobiography *The Confessions* that stealing fruit showed the signs of fallen human nature. I pulled out all my childhood antics as evidence of the same. Every deed marked us for condemnation. We were two black guys—me in Buffalo and he in Northern Africa—pointing out the always present and basic need for salvation: no innocence, only latent depravity, behind the words and deeds of even the young.

For my mother, joining the church was the beginning of God's work in my life; she believed God marked me for a special purpose. Why else would I be here despite the odds against me being born healthy?

Miracle baby, indeed!

My extended family was more than willing to play along with this assessment. So, it wasn't long before people in and outside my extended family referred to me as the professor or the preacher. The full reason for this was not clear to me, and I didn't push for more details, more explanation, and more evidence. Both were roles I would eventually embrace, and it felt pretty good to have people thinking so highly of me.

There was little that connected someone my age to either title, but it seemed to really say "Here's a kid who goes to church, seems to respect adults, stays out of major trouble, and does well in school . . . he's got to achieve middle-class and important African American community status." Two long-standing markers of this status are the ministry and the academy—preacher and teacher. In African American history, some of the figures remembered with great fondness held advanced degrees, were ministers, were educators, or both and were in this regard understood as community leaders, including Anna J. Cooper, Benjamin Mays, Bishop Barbara Harris, Martin L. King Jr., Rev. Dr. Pauli Murray, to name a few.

There was no reason to believe I'd rise to the stature of any of these people, but in my community, like most communities exposed to both the promise and pitfalls of racialized life, it didn't take that level of achievement to be marked "special." People were proud for less lofty gains than that; the ability to point to someone they knew as having "made it" was enough. These assumptions concerning my future status set me apart, gave me special attention—and who doesn't want to be noticed and appreciated for talents and gifts, whether imagined or real?

Whatever we mean by identity is shaped early, and this type of affirmation certainly helped to give mine context and purpose that connected me to a larger whole.

Working myself into the church and its claim on my life meant embracing my mother, honoring her hopes for her family, and seeing myself as someone with purpose and importance in a cosmic sense.

Chapter Three

CHURCH IS IN WALKING DISTANCE

Monumental achievements in life weren't necessary, but for my mother, education was of fundamental importance.

In my immediate family everyone went to school, even though they didn't all finish. My brother, Raymond (or "Ray Ray," as we called him), was only a semester or so away from completing his undergraduate degree when he decided to leave school and pursue money, good times, and what life could offer beyond the religiously informed options presented by my mother. My sister Linda, the youngest girl, went to nursing school, and my oldest sister, Joyce, was the real intellect in the family, as she went to both college and graduate school, read Latin, and went on to work on a doctorate. She didn't complete the doctorate; money and the sexism of the department in which she studied made that a painfully long process, ultimately resulting in an incomplete dissertation.

Joyce pushed her love of books and learning on me—and resisting wasn't as easy as I would have liked. Because she was older and had a student's schedule, there were times she was responsible for watching me, and on those days, she made me learn a new word and use it correctly in a sentence.

She gave me books and made me read and circle the words I didn't know. I'd have to look them up later. Appreciating what she was doing for me was difficult, and that informal homeschooling didn't strike in me a great love for formal education. It did, however, expose me to a world of ideas, to a sense that the meaning of things and the importance of ideas extended beyond my block. She, very early, showed me that there were wonders—whether I understood or appreciated them mattered little—and human creativity beyond the doctrines, creeds, and rituals of my church experience. Early on, Joyce set in place a useful tension between learning and faith.

Image 4. The author (second row, fifth from left) in his second-grade class photograph.

The desk for study wasn't tucked away in the corner of a bedroom. It was against the wall in the "living room," the same room that housed our television. Joyce, during the times she lived at home and was still in school, spread out on the couch where she wrote or edited her assignments and graded papers for courses she taught. When I was young, I had one of those old schoolhouse desks with the inkwell near the door separating the kitchen and the living room. It was near the window looking into the backyard opposite my father's La-Z-Boy chair. I'd sit there and color or draw, and with time I'd do my schoolwork at the big desk.

While I didn't like my sister's lessons, there was something about the company of adults I enjoyed. I had little interest in children my own age. I didn't like preschool; the idea of forced naps on randomly assigned blankets, followed by someone else combing my hair rubbed me wrong. And so I complained about preschool until something had to be done. To accommodate my wishes, my father switched shifts so he could watch me during the day, but there were also times when my mother took me to school with her.

My mother enrolled at Rosary Hill College after I was born. Joyce also attended the school, but she was a more advanced student than my mother was. I have faint memories of my sister tutoring my mother and limited recollection of exactly what my mother studied, although she would eventually take a job as a hospital administrator.

Some years later, when I was older and knew the right questions to ask, my mother told me she went to school in order to provide more for her children. Getting an education and gaining economic power made my father and his thinking less impactful on her and her children. She got a degree—long after her parents first made the opportunity available—and she used it to make opportunities available that wouldn't have been otherwise. Over time, my mother's plan meant most to me. My siblings were already carving out their independence and had some critical distance, and so the familial situation had less impact on them. I was the only one of the children living full-time in the house (although my brother and older sister would move in and out for a while).

I had examples of people securing an education and some sense of what an education could mean in real-life circumstance, but even with this I don't recall enjoying school when it was my turn to go.

There was no particularly traumatic experience that turned me against institutions of formal learning; I just didn't care for anything related to school. This was only complicated at Public School No. 74, the local grade school in my neighborhood. Some of the teachers lived in the neighborhood, including one of my aunt's sisters who lived around the corner from us in a house that looked like it belonged in the suburbs. But many of them commuted to the inner city, and, from the way they talked to us, it seemed they believed news reports and anecdotes about people in the 'hood.

I was in school when physical punishment was still permitted, and it was used to keep the unruly in line. Even the new teachers, fresh out of school, used corporal punishment—a hit on the knuckles with a ruler—to keep us in line.

The idea that we should be hit with a ruler or belt because of infractions of the rules didn't sit well with all my classmates. A classmate with a stutter was one of the first to rebel against this practice. I think he'd been caught talking, and the teacher—a young white woman—called him to the front of the class and started to give him licks with a ruler. Fitzgerald told her to stop: "St-st-stop hitting me!" She didn't, so that little boy grabbed the ruler and hit her.

I remember the teacher running out of the room screaming. She came back with help, and Fitzgerald was marked a troublemaker for as long as I remained at that school. I don't know what eventually happened to him. He may have become successful or, like some of the others from my childhood, he may have died too young.

That seemed to be the approach to dealing with the students: contain us and reward those who don't cause trouble, who are quiet and do what they are told. I fell into that group. I didn't cause much trouble or at least wasn't caught very often. I did my work, although I never enjoyed it.

The teachers and the administrators at the school had low expectations—dreams for us that didn't extend beyond the limitations of the inner city; if we stayed out of trouble we could secure respectable employment, stay out of prison, have a family and a relatively good life. It was easy to fall through the gaps, and few would care, particularly if the student didn't have involved parents or family examples of educational success. Even this care and these examples could be challenged. It was a fragile process staying visible without being in trouble.

In grade school, I started having trouble with my eyes. From what I remember, it just seemed that I couldn't recognize particular words, and I dreaded group reading when everyone would have to read out loud. I just thought I couldn't read well. One of my friends would sometimes whisper words to me, but it was just as likely he'd take that opportunity to increase his teacher praise by picking up where I had to leave off—"Very good" would be the response to his reading.

My mother was concerned, but like most parents, she assumed that the authority of the school was accurate. They thought I just wasn't very good, that I wasn't very gifted. If it wasn't for the guidance counselor, that argument might have been enough. But he suggested my mother think about another school or at the very least have my eyes checked. She did both—the second as an afterthought. She investigated transferring me to one of the Catholic schools. The response was to have my eyes checked first. The result? I needed glasses.

My "Clark Kent" of Superman fame eyeglass frames in a dark, almost black color solved the problem but got some laughs, even from the teacher—a real disappointment for me. Kids will laugh, sure. But should an adult, the teacher, join in the laughter as I walked late into the classroom?

I could see now, but I was losing interest in school. The guidance counselor again came to the rescue: "Your son is bored; these classes aren't a challenge for him. Get him out of here before he loses all interest in learning."

Until that could be arranged, he'd take me out of class at times and provide activities meant to keep me motivated and away from the unimaginative approach to education that marked my formal classroom. The guidance counselor's conversation with my mother and his efforts to keep me from total boredom coincided with the city's new initiative: "special progress" programs that brought gifted students together. After a few years at No. 74, I transferred to the special progress program housed at Public School No. 81. That school was still in the city of Buffalo but was on the north side of the city—with a stronger economic base, better homes, and a type of ease to life.

The whole arrangement was different: we exchanged classes and had a particular teacher for each subject; we were also isolated from the general classes, not even recess or lunch was held with the students not marked "gifted." We only saw them on the bus to school and the bus home.

I still didn't enjoy school, but it was more of a challenge. The classes were diverse, with more than the black kids from the neighborhood, and the teachers pushed us and expected excellence. The homework and projects involved late nights, as both my mother and Joyce helped me with writing assignments, macaroni maps, and papier-mâché creations.

There was curiosity. It was that curiosity that got me invitations for play dates with some of my classmates. Many of them had only encountered blacks on television, and my encounters with whites were not much more substantial, with a few exceptions; namely my mother's friend Candy, who, with my mother, was a member of "Mended Hearts," an organization for people who'd had open-heart surgery.

Outside church, I had never thought of my mother as a joiner, but I was glad she was a part of this group. I liked their gatherings, the adults who gave me so much attention, and I thought the world of Candy—my first big friend. I'd spend some weekends with Candy and her mother.

I enjoyed the time away with these two women who loved me and who were different in worldview and features. Coming home was difficult after that time spent with Candy. We were so close that when she finally married, her fiancé talked with me about it and, with grace and compassion, asked my permission. Outside Candy and a few others, I encountered whites on television, in stores, as repair guys, and as the occasional visitor to our church. I knew as little about them as they knew about me.

Image 5. The author as a child, with family friend Candy.

They lived in different parts of town, and from what I heard and could see, it seemed they, in general, had more things and finer homes. I assumed life was easier for them in certain ways, but also—perhaps—less high-spirited. I didn't think they had as much fun in church because white kids didn't get to see adults jump around, happy to know the Lord. Their preachers, I didn't think, preached like ours—loud, energetic, with so much passion and the ability to weave stories out of a book with such odd words in it. But I liked Candy and other whites I met.

It seemed our two communities didn't get along. I gathered that much from conversations I'd overheard and bits of information from television, including the tragic assassination of Dr. Martin L. King Jr. and the heat surrounding it. But at Public School No. 81, we shared space, and for the most part offenses were minor.

On rare occasions the external world impinged on us, like when the local white supremacist group threatened schoolchildren and we were forced to have recess inside amid rumors that young black children had been attacked and hurt by this group. Teachers didn't correct our thinking about this group and its danger, and I didn't know what to make of it and its activities. I, like my classmates, was frightened, but that was a level of racism beyond my typical encounters.

What I usually dealt with were the "you're pretty smart" type of comments at school that included an undercurrent of surprise, or the repairman who remarked how clean our house was, as if we should be living in squalor. My mother met those comments with sarcasm and her own questions concerning the condition of the other person's home. "Of course my home is clean and well appointed . . . are you surprised because your home isn't?" I took it all in stride for the most part.

Those subtle challenges to my intellect didn't push me to prove anything to my teachers and classmates. I had enough motivation and high enough expectations from family, who donned me "the professor," to not be moved by those remarks.

I did well because it was a community expectation. I didn't enjoy reading, but my sister had conditioned me, so I knew I had to either read or fake it well. I didn't get lost in the stories of children's literature and the great classics she brought to my attention. Books at that point were flat to me, and I had to wrestle through the words. When I imagined new worlds and me in them, it was the result of pretending to be a superhero with my dog as my sidekick or the long-lost sixth member of the Jackson Five, whose voice and dancing ability added something very special to the group.

I wasn't the only African American in my special progress world, but there were only a handful of us, as I remember it. And while many of the white students walked home, we rode public transportation to get back to our neighborhoods. We were "bused"—that questionable move that shuffled the political deck without radically changing the cultural sensibilities undergirding race-based education.

The kids in the books we read bore little resemblance to us in appearance and experience. Activities and questions of life that motivated and challenged the main characters in so many of the stories guiding our learning had little to do with our life stories. This is not to say that we were the victims of profound poverty and blight. That wasn't it at all. Rather, so much of what qualified as knowledge did not include our families and histories. American history quickly glossed over the trauma of enslavement and keyed in on the typical figures, like Martin L. King Jr., but left out his more aggressive political critiques.

We, at least during Black History Month, heard stories of great African Americans who had helped to transform the United States. But all too often these stories were disconnected from the rest of the year and did not take up much ink within our textbooks. They were footnotes in a way, peppering history as we were taught it, without deep roots in the life of the country. It wouldn't be until college that African American letters became a part of the fundamental language of learning and culture for me, and where the thinking of African Americans played a role in what it meant to be educated.

Yet mine wasn't the experience of Malcolm X: no one blatantly told me what I couldn't be—and it would be some years (high school, in fact)—before I would be called a "nigger" within the context of my formal education. And had there been that type of encounter, it wouldn't have mattered much, in that the church was shaping my sense of vocational possibilities and prospects more so than the school and its cast of characters. After all, I looked like a preacher . . . no, maybe a professor.

I, and my family, assumed I would receive an education, that I was entitled to it—whether I enjoyed it or not—and that I should perform well regardless of what others thought or might imply.

It was television that forced the most engaged race conversation of my young years through the miniseries *Roots*. My school wasn't the only one set ablaze with talk about race as a consequence of Alex Haley's 1976 novel turned television saga. The man who guided Malcolm X through his autobiography was now further shaping public imagination by humanizing his enslaved ancestors. His personal story was our story, the story of a whole community, and it gave us a way of venting against discrimination. What is more, it forced whites around me to acknowledge injustice.

Although an official apology for slavery would take much longer (and repayment for labor isn't really on the Washington, DC, agenda) individuals lamented the roles their families played in the enslavement of Africans and regretted (without giving it back) the wealth accumulated through this injustice. Even those without any visible wealth recognized the nature of their privilege, and if nothing else the miniseries provided an opportunity for conversation.

In my school, we had formal sessions to discuss slavery and what it meant to the United States in the light of our viewing *Roots*, and we students had our own, unofficial exchanges. First, there was some embarrassment on the part of African Americans that they had been slaves, but that quickly gave way to anger and recognition that the source of all the misery we encountered was not ourselves. Haley wasn't the first to say this. No, the Nation of Islam, very much present in my home of Buffalo, attempted to instill this knowledge, but most African Americans found its theology too fantastic, too foreign, and their practices and ethics too militaristic. Black churches in some ways also fought this battle but ultimately clouded the issue with talk of individual salvation that pushed followers beyond this world and its history. In school it was different. There was none of this theologizing as a way of covering discomfort. Our teachers were trying to use this story and the anxiety it generated as a pedagogical moment, to finally educate beyond anecdotes and stereotypes.

All the jokes in my neighborhood about white people, all the lines we thought so funny from comedian Redd Foxx about white people and their habits, we connected to *Roots*. Foxx's character Fred Sanford, on the sitcom *Sanford and Son*, enters a home in Beverly Hills to collect some items for his junkyard, but he defuses the privilege and awe of wealth—signifies the difference between his junk and their riches—with a simple, humorous comment: "White people's houses smell like lettuce." In other words, they are nondescript and lack the aromas of life. Instead, their private spaces are marked by a sense of something missing. Knowing the smells of food and the sounds coming from our own homes, this comment of Fred Sanford's made us laugh knowingly. "Yep, that's right!" was a common response to Sanford's remark. It's somewhat embarrassing now to admit this, but this Redd Foxx joke was an inside joke told publicly, and without much supporting information. We wondered how things had progressed from the land encountered by Kunta Kinte, Haley's ancestor, played by LeVar Burton, to the observation made by Fred Sanford. How could physical trauma and humor both tell the story of black and white interaction?

In my neighborhood, we often thought in terms of two histories intertwined, but rarely were these histories interrogated for a shared complexity beyond the more easily identified but superficial links. *Roots* forced a confrontation with what it meant in the United States to be black or to be white, as well as the legacy of that difference. And it gave vitality to the trauma inflicted by means of that difference.

I always knew that I was black and that being black had particular connotations in this country, but Alex Haley gave that recognition a charge and layered it with a particular importance because the personal is political. He, through that miniseries, chronicled African Americans' pride of place in this country hard won over the course of centuries.

Even church was a bit different post-*Roots*. While the impact of the miniseries didn't turn my church in the direction of Africa through a blending of nonbiblical but deeply African rituals and theologies, it did add a bit of historical narrative to our assumptions of specialness. Haley gave my church, and churches like it, a way to point out what we perceived as the truth of our religious claims: "God has brought us from a mighty long way."

Outside of church, we sometimes walked around my neighborhood thinking about the characters from *Roots* while mimicking James Brown: "Say It Loud—I'm

Black and I'm Proud." This expression of pride and importance produced a certain type of ease, an indescribable recognition of our black bodies beyond (and more positive than) what we were taught in church. At times it took the form of just a smile or a spring in my step—small activities, to be sure—but something about that smile or step placed me squarely in life and gave me awareness of my presence and my body. It was an awareness of my body as having meaning and purpose, not simply that thing keeping me from complete devotion to God. My body, if Haley was to be believed, was more than a vessel of sin.

There were cultural markers of the importance of our personhood that cut against the social pressure to be beautiful by being different than we were—different hair (less kinky), different eyes (less brown), and different skin (lighter). Yet, both in my neighborhood and in the larger world, the messages were mixed—an odd blend of appreciation and dislike.

Too many times, even after the revelation of *Roots*, I was called "white boy" by my neighborhood friends because of the freckles on my hands and face (I resembled my mother), the reddish patches of hair on my head, and because I did well in school. For my playmates, to succeed in the white world of academics was to surrender to whiteness—whatever that meant—and to give into white social standards and expectations. No one in my neighborhood really had in-depth conversations about the culture of "whiteness"—the signs and symbols, the meta-narrative of supremacy, and the genealogy of racism, as Cornel West described some years later.

They didn't raise questions concerning the source of this hierarchy of beauty or why black people had a tendency to reject some of the signs of success (outside sports and entertainment) and whites claimed them as their own. The conversations weren't that deep. It was just the way people thought and the way things were. My friends saw the markers of what they perceived as whiteness, and they responded. I, because of my dedication to my schoolwork, was surrendering my blackness, the thing that made us different and that marked our psychological territory.

Unfortunately, blackness, for them, was anything but success—unless you could play football or basketball or entertain people. I would learn to call this condition internalized racism.

What I encountered in my neighborhood was self-suspicion in its most awkward and graphic form, but it wasn't the only way it shadowed my world. Whether recognized or not wasn't the point; race and racism factored into life. Their sensual signs were always there in the large and small events of life— even in the activities of a child.

Although I don't remember race-related conversations between members of my father's family, I imagine they had mixed feelings toward who they were, although I assume they respected their heritage and communicated this in some particular ways. I just don't remember well enough the time I spent with them to be able to recall with any certainty. However, my mother's family was closer and more involved in my daily life, and I remember her family's pride of heritage. At the same time, I must admit, my grandmother— matriarch of the family—was "color-struck": having a preference for people light in complexion. She, like some members of her immediate family, could easily pass for white—straight hair, pale complexion, and fairly light eyes. However, she chose not to pass, as far as I know, and she married a dark man, suggesting no desire to blend into white society. She clearly saw beauty in a dark complexion.

Despite this, it wasn't uncommon for my grandmother to make disparaging remarks concerning dark-skinned men and women her grandchildren brought to visit. These unkind remarks were odd in that her children represented different shades—from very light to dark. She was kind to and gentle with those she knew by blood—dark or even darker than dark—but those outside this immediate circle received an informal version of the color test. My mother also had this tendency with people my siblings and I brought home: "She sure is dark" or "You like them dark" weren't uncommon remarks regarding the women my brother loved or some of the women I thought I loved through the years. To add to this tangled mess, my grandmother, mother, and other members of my extended family weren't any more comfortable with whites brought "home," although they did become accepting of some over the years.

My family's final criterion for inclusion in their world seemed comfort with us—a willingness and ability to find one's fit in the extended family and to protect that fit and that family. Each person seemed to have a role to play, and as long as they stayed in that role things worked well, or problems could at least be pushed below the surface, only emerging in whispered tones. Indiscretions could be explained or overlooked in some cases, as long as there was a general allegiance to the family. Ultimately, that commitment trumped the "look" of the people sharing this bond.

It was a comfortable group—as long as you didn't ask too many questions or dig too deep—with its own particular idiosyncrasies and shortcomings, as well as its strong points. Any family member's house could be home for the day or week, and any family member's table could be a place for a meal. Sleepovers with cousins were more like going to bed at home. Everyone tried to maintain this approach, but my mother went out of her way to help family whenever possible—including opening our home to cousins who needed to stay with us in our small house for unspecified lengths of time. At times her kindness was taken advantage of, but she would chalk this up to Christian duty, with a reward at another time and in accordance with God's will. This wasn't my father's attitude. But even if I can't say much about my father, I can say he went along with these additional costs, these inconveniences, for an extended family to which he was not close.

For me, it meant I wasn't the only kid in the house. There were play-mates, distractions, and a network of relationships for someone who felt alone at times because of the age difference between my siblings and me. These house guests and I didn't always get along, but there was a sense of togeth-erness—and a stern warning from my mother or father—that forced us to move beyond friction. There was a network of discipline, because any aunt or uncle—any adult, really—could reprimand or reward.

Despite my interest in and time around my cousins, I didn't really like being around kids. My cousins were the exception that tended to prove the rule. People in general were prone to ask questions I found intrusive or at least time-consuming, and they were questions that pushed me beyond my comfort zone of interaction. They made assumptions concerning my interests and probed into my life to find the fit between what they thought and what I thought. As a child I was aware of this—the tendency of adults to meddle and talk down as if life somehow eluded children.

I've always been an introvert, more comfortable away from crowds. I told jokes and clowned around with family and my small network of friends, but this hid me from them more than it exposed things about me. The jokes or the goofy walk didn't tell them much about what I thought, my fears about my mother's health, or my anxiety over my parents' unstable relationship. I tried to keep them too busy laughing to ask me many questions.

This confession about being an introvert has been met with some resistance or at least confusion—"No, not you! You don't seem that way, and you're a preacher!" But I've always wondered if that response says more about the shocked person (How can a kid not like to be with other kids, or a preacher not like being around people?) than it does about me. Whatever the right answer is, this preference for my own company, time and space away from people, has always been a part of me, even when in the church.

My family and my church involved relationships with people even when not physically present, and I found something about this difficult. It wasn't that I preferred the company of books, and, while I loved television, it wasn't that television prevented me from developing social skills. I had these skills as far as I can remember, but it seemed a bit tedious. I was a loner at times of necessity because of my age in relationship to my siblings, but I was also outgoing at other times when the situation required it. Yet something about it all made me a bit uncomfortable. If I was not with my small group of friends, I much preferred my mother's company, and taunts of "mama's boy" did little to change this. Being close to her was comfortable and gave me a bit of ease from my fear that in my absence she might become ill or go to the hospital and I wouldn't know it and couldn't help. There was good reason behind this thinking.

During a church trip to the Palmira Rock pageant celebrating certain dimensions of the Mormon story, my mother became ill. My siblings rode the bus back to Buffalo. I was determined to stay with my mother, and no one could change my mind. It's a blur—people trying to comfort me, to take me away from my mother so she could be treated. No, not without me, it wasn't going to happen. I wanted to stay with her, be around her, see her and hear her voice. Despite the surroundings or the problem of her health, being near her gave me some comfort, and I'm sure I assumed it did something for her as well. There was something about just being present—knowing what was taking place that was important to me. But to stay around and not be sent back to Buffalo, I had to cover up some of my fear and dread. If I seemed too emotional, people might make me leave. So, I had to be conscious of my facial expressions and how much information I provided through my expressions and words. I had to be a stoic little kid.

Episodes like this taught me lessons I've held to and express through my tendency toward what most would call pessimism and what I prefer to call worldly realism. I prepare for the worse and expect it from most people—except, at times, those closest to me—and if it doesn't happen I am pleasantly surprised but always ready for worst-case scenarios to manifest. People can use your vulnerability against you. Even the nicest people; those who seem most on your side, can do this. So . . . beware, be careful.

I became—and if I am honest, I continue to be—suspicious with a reluctance to trust and a deep sensitivity to being wronged (particularly being wronged without retribution). I protect myself. Tied to this sensibility were the words of my grandfather: "God doesn't require us to be fools." Never let people know exactly what you are thinking or feeling; this much I think I picked up from my father, despite my mother's opinions to the contrary in light of her church-based sensibilities. I must admit, there was something of subtle comfort in being part of a church community that prayed for my family, expressed concern for my mother, and tried to provide relief through wise words about the righteous prospering. Yet I remained suspicious and guarded.

This posture toward people and relationships isn't exactly what one might expect from a person who claimed that God looks after the righteous, but there was also something about it that was authentic to my religion. People are flawed and prone to deceit and bad faith in their dealings. The difference, however, was supposed to be a Christian's willingness to turn the other cheek, to embrace people and move beyond human fault. Doing this was an opportunity to show that the righteous will prevail and that their victory might just bring sinners to Christ.

All this posturing raised a question. A concise but powerful question: where was God in all this? Why allow my mother—a good Christian—to go through these ups and downs? And why all the other mess encountered by church people?

I certainly didn't have sophisticated answers, but I thought that if I threw myself into the stories about Jesus, maybe I could find something that would tame the questions. I often looked at the stained glass windows in my church, trying to catch the eye of the Jesus who looked nothing like me. Perhaps in the scenes of his interactions with children about my size there was something that would ease my tensions and fears? Maybe in a dream Jesus would tell me something that would make a difference, a kind word from God given me in the middle of the night? Andráe Crouch, the musician who gave gospel music a bit of funk, sang that Jesus is the answer, and I hoped Jesus would show me some kindness and make that musical proclamation real in my life. I, like others in my church, wanted to see the hand of God in everything taking place, and we assumed God's will pushed the faithful in a positive direction.

The mothers of the church—the older women, often widows, who informally directed the thinking and activities of the church—sang, "I am weak and I need thy strength and power to help me over my weakest hour. Lead me through the darkness thy face to see, lead me, oh Lord, lead me." And I sang along, swaying to the sound of the music and trying to understand the words. Like novelist Richard Wright in *Black Boy*, who experienced at a young age his grandmother's church activities including the music, I, too, was moved by the church's music. I wanted it to be some type of response to my personal needs—that the authors of the song's lyrics knew something about me, although we'd never met.

I felt assured by the closeness of human bodies, the people around me holding my hands as we closed our eyes and swayed to the music. But unlike Wright, who found the world more pressing and compelling than the church, I surrendered to the church. I allowed myself to believe what I was told, despite the ways in which it conflicted with the world around me. At the very least, I let the stuff of church life occupy my mind and time in ways that kept my mother's health and my parents' unhappy marriage from consuming me.

My siblings were older and more insulated from the drama of my home than I was, but I had the church and I welcomed it. That building and its activities served as a type of respite from the stresses of family life, to the extent a child could understand those stresses. In church I didn't have to think about the arguments in the middle of the night my parents didn't think I heard. Tears of joy replaced my mother's periodic tears over the pictures of her son Kenny, gone too young, dressed in his suit and lying, eyes closed, in his casket. For a few hours I could forget those sad tears shed in front of the son who should not have been born, a "surprise" child who would naturally feel a responsibility to lessen the sadness and be enough to bring a smile. I was told I'd been born to make a difference, to comfort, but I didn't see how that could be true when my mother cried those sad tears or when I heard the muffled sounds of my parents arguing.

Chapter Four

DOC' IN THE PULPIT

Our little church on Northland Avenue eventually became affiliated with the African Methodist Episcopal (AME) Church, the oldest black denomination in the country.

The dynamics of the church changed with this push into the AME denomination. Local autonomy was lost because bishops, with each bishop managing a geographical area called an Episcopal District, ran the denomination. My church, Agape AME Church, was in the first district. It was the oldest of all the districts and the home of "Mother Bethel," the first church in the denomination pastored by the founding leader, Richard Allen.

This move into a formal denomination gave some a sense of security by putting the survival of the church on broader shoulders. But some left the church out of protest against this move into a large and bureaucratic organization without the same family feel and freedom of belief and practice. For them, this affiliation worked against the basic idea behind the congregation, which had been started in a home in the 1960s by a group that left Delaine-Warring AME Church in order to do things their way.

From its period of independence through its affiliation with the AME denomination, Agape had a variety of pastors. It was with one of these ministers in particular that my formal participation in the church increased in significant ways.

Reverend Hudson (so much time has passed that I don't recall his first name) was an understated and dignified minister. His hallmark was the complete sermon manuscript; there was no straying from his written word on

Sundays when he was in the pulpit. I will never forget one Sunday when Reverend Hudson, a dark-skinned, small-of-stature and husky man, prepared to preach his sermon. Glasses on, flowing black robe properly positioned, shoes shining . . . everything was in place. Except for the correct sermon.

As he began, Hudson realized that he had the wrong manuscript. Without saying much other than announcing the mistake, he walked out of the pulpit and went into his office on the left of the pulpit, grabbed the correct manuscript from his bag (literally a paper bag from a grocery store) of sermons, and moved back to the pulpit.

Manuscript on the pulpit, robe still flowing, he began again. That misstep spoke volumes: What about inspiration for preaching sermons? What exactly did he do in preparation, and didn't he check the title on that manuscript before service started? How far back in his ministry did the contents of the bag go? What got him started storing up sermons that way in the first place?

He wasn't the most dynamic preacher in Buffalo, New York. Hudson wouldn't win any preaching contests or cut any albums full of inspirational sermons. But he was the pastor and my Sunday school teacher.

Sunday school was often taught by members of the congregation who were committed to it as a form of ministry. In smaller churches, like Agape, even the pastor held this duty. Don't assume Jesus restricted his special knowledge and interpretative skills to other adults. No, he taught the kids. "Let the children come unto me" is what Jesus said to those trying to keep the preteens away from him. Reverend Hudson seemed in this case to practice what Jesus preached.

I didn't enjoy going to Sunday school because I thought I knew more than the members of the class, and being with them, with their silly questions and comments, was a waste of time. My mother didn't see it that way, and so I attended.

Some thought of Sunday school as a shift in focus from the concerns of the "world" to the wisdom of the faith. In this way, it prepared Christians to empty themselves into Sunday worship with few mental distractions.

Sunday school and Sunday worship are the church's version of the "reboot," a spiritual tune-up of the mind meant to open and sensitize people to the truth and soul-edifying meaning of the songs, prayers, and sermon. However, people didn't think this because these Sunday lessons were tailored to my church and the sociocultural community it represented.

Companies produced the books we used, but they were for the generic Christian—just like department stores sell clothing based on a "general" American body type. Until some years later when my church began to purchase culturally sensitive materials, few of the children pictured looked like us or spoke like us. None of the kids on those pages described good as "bad" or "funky" as pleasant. The kids in those books didn't wonder about being black and proud; they didn't have to think about race at all.

The lessons had to be altered, retro-fit for our context. In my case, this meant changing examples from Jim and Jane, whose lives revolved around the dynamics of the suburbs, to the life circumstances of the inner city. And, although our neighborhood was fairly secure, with people who more often than not looked out for each other and raised children with a sense of community responsibilities, we weren't in the suburbs. Unlike Jim and Jane's home as portrayed in the Sunday school materials, my neighborhood was an area of contradictions, fledgling gangs and college campuses; blue-collar workers near the expressway that took the lawyers, politicians, and business leaders to the downtown offices; illness within a short distance from hospitals; relatively poor public schools with limited energy and vision for creative learning near elite private schools for the wealthy and/or gifted.

What we encountered was different in so many ways from the lives of the kids we read about in our Sunday school materials, and Sunday school teachers in churches like mine had to figure out how to bring together the Bible and our life circumstances. Often this was done through questions: "What does this lesson on the 23rd Psalm tell you?" Or, "What is the Lord trying to tell us through this scripture?" And we'd answer by applying biblical claims to our little lives using schoolyard examples like neighborhood squabbles with friends as well as poorly told family stories. The stuff was mundane, tame if compared to what the adults could report about their lives, but it was what we had to offer to those questions about the Bible and us.

One Sunday morning, as we were sitting in a circle, Reverend Hudson went around the room asking each student what he or she wanted to be when an adult. Many talked about being a doctor, lawyer . . . what children typically say. I said that I wanted to be a preacher when I grew up. I don't recall contemplating what I would say as other children spoke their dreams. And my proclamation wasn't simply one-upmanship because there were other options—like president of the United States—that would trump what most in the room said about their futures.

I don't remember exactly how old I was at the time, but I was young enough for the announcement to become news. An adult feeling a calling to ministry was rather common, although the person might not follow through on the initial energetic claim. But a child . . . that was a different story—something special, with a type of innocence of motive that had to be appreciated and cherished.

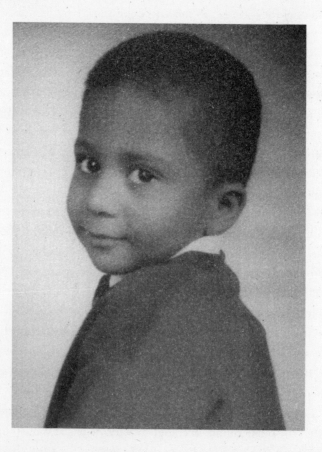

Image 6. The author as a small child.

I don't think my only concern was securing Reverend Hudson's approval, although what child doesn't want the attention of adults, particularly adults with the type of community and spiritual authority held by the preacher? Perhaps I thought this announcement would set me apart, give me a larger role in some type of spiritual drama. Whatever the motivation for my announcement, Reverend Hudson took it seriously. He began my training in ministry shortly after I made that proclamation.

You can imagine what this might mean to a preteen. It provided a sense of purpose, a sense of place that belonged to me, that defined something important about me. It was something to shoot for in a world where each person must belong to something, as James Baldwin put it years ago in *Go Tell It on the Mountain*.

In addition to securing the favor of leaders like Hudson, my venture into the pulpit, as it was for Baldwin, may have been my effort to claim a type of authority over my father and other adults. They had years, had experience, but I would have a calling—a direct line to salvation and the ability to dispense the secrets of the "Good News" to others. There was little within my home that I could control or determine, but ministry would give me an importance beyond my years, an ability to talk beyond my limited experience and have people take to heart what I said.

Whatever my motivations, there is an important question that should be asked in hindsight: why would this minister, this experienced preacher with his own calling, take so seriously the babblings of a child? Was his positive response more about him and his desire for a protégée? I was just another kid in Sunday school, but did Hudson want to claim me as a "son" in the ministry for whatever reason? He had children, but none of them were involved in ministry at the church. Perhaps he saw me as someone he could groom for the pastorate in ways he might never do with his own sons? Maybe he was just a nice guy who didn't want to crush the aspirations of a young African American male? Or were the standards for inclusion in the ministry really that low? One just needs to claim it, and it's yours?

There was and continues to be a privileging of the "call" to ministry as a subjective and individual response to what people assume is the urging of a divine force. No one saw the interaction between the person called and the

God doing the calling. There were booming announcements from "on high," no changes in a person's appearance—like the graying of Moses's hair after contact with God. Preachers wore suits, but anyone could buy a suit. And they carried Bibles, but everyone in the church had a Bible.

Ministers talk about their work as a "yes" to God's demand for their service. But the validity of this process was checked only based on the outcomes of a person's ministry. Did the person called *seem* to do work that might suggest God's favor? Outside of this approach, criteria were vague and shifting. And, in a more general sense, what people thought about someone's call seemed to have more to do with the sociocultural "look" and fit of the person into the role than anything really measurable.

For as long as there have been independent black churches, ministry has been something of a prestigious position within African American communities. The person called to ministry was believed to have greater sensitivity to the workings of the spirit world, a direct line to God, and greater insight into life, along with the power to transform lives.

There was no formal age requirement imposed systematically in that God was believed to select whomever God selected and this could be the most unlikely of characters—the boy David used to defeat the giant Goliath, or the humble but fiery Nat Turner, who sparked terror in the name of God. I didn't think I was the equivalent of any of these towering figures of religious history, although every Christian hopes for a special role in God's plan. To be like them, to mirror the significance of their accomplishments, wasn't the standard even when a person seemed to exhibit *special* closeness to God.

Truth be told, the preacher syndrome is such a strange arrangement. There is clearly something of ego in this calling, but it is shrouded by an appeal to God. The human ego is in synergy with divine presumptiveness, played through a sense of original sin. It isn't that the would-be minister is worthy, but that God is merciful and can use imperfection to bring about wonders. This easily and often goes to the head of ministers, and they come to see themselves as indispensable to the project—the one without whom God's plan might fail.

I don't know that Hudson and the others he told about my proclamation had particularly high expectations for me—other than training me to be a good representative of the faith. Why would they? Wasn't it enough to want to follow the leading of the Lord? God would figure out exactly what my role should be in that work. As long as I put God first, any task given me as a minister was an important task.

Mindful of this, it wasn't my age so much that might give people pause. In fact, it might demonstrate to many the power of God to work through even one so young and inexperienced. No boldness on my part—just a kid sitting in a room who said ministry sounds as good as firefighting, police work, or medicine. They all deal with people—monitoring (or destroying) health. Nonetheless, it was important for the person "called" to have a narrative about the draw of God on his (typically "his") life. Every minister had a story of calling, of the point at which they could fight no more and had to surrender life to God and the church: "Not my will, but thy will be done," said with eyes turned upward.

My story?

Nothing spectacular. No beams of light through the window, no breeze from the wings of angels felt by all present. There wasn't the drama of Moses being assigned the deliverance of an important people, or the Apostle Paul knocked off a horse as the voice of the Christ calls to him for a life change. But it was what I had: "What do you want to be when you grow up?" . . . "A preacher."

The boy was becoming a *man* of God.

The boy/man dichotomy is important here because there was something deeply masculine about church and church ministry. This was the case in most black churches, not just my church. So much about the structure, the organization, the doctrine and creeds of churches like mine pushed the dominance of men in subtle and also not so subtle ways.

The Bible is a patriarchal book, its stories told from the perspective of men, and the key figures—not always, but by and large—are men. The assumed savior of the world for Christians—God in human form—comes as a male, and his disciples (those recognized as such by most people) were men, and these men determined the rules and regulations for the fledgling Christian community so as to privilege men.

Mindful of all of this and in an effort to mirror the early followers of Jesus, black Christian communities have largely maintained this same male-centered leadership. Of course, there are exceptions to this rule. But the continued fight against sexism in churches suggests people within black churches—men and women—when convenient still pull out of their bag of spiritual tricks the age-old argument that the Bible demands male leadership within the religious community, and to step outside the demands of the Bible would entail rejection of God's plan for the saved and the divine design for human community writ large.

Men in the church are grateful to be men, and both men and women see restrictive practices as natural in that they are based on physical limitations and divine law. Gender roles were set by spiritual commitment to the faith, and they were fixed or reified through church theology—a kind of "owner's manual" for the faithful that indicated why and how each saved person fit into the larger whole of the church.

When I first announced my interest in ministry, I was much too young to play this gender game to great effect. I observed it, and in simplistic ways could describe its contours. I was being groomed to take my rightful place within this system. If nothing else, I was a religious-sexist-homophobic-with-biblical-and-theological-justifications-in-training.

As part of this education I was learning the language of sin and imperfection—learning by rote to recite God's demands in this regard but without more than the ability to mimic at this point. I was being taught to decipher and guard masculinity of Christians as soldiers "marching to war" with God as a ruling Lord and King!

Men who didn't walk just right or who exhibited any "hint" of being gay, or women who didn't readily accept second-class status had their salvation brought into question. The church expected them to accept this arrangement as their lot in spiritual life and as the payment necessary for a relationship with the black church community. Some kept their deepest secrets just that—secret.

Everyone in the church had his or her secrets that were shared only in silent prayer—or, for the daring few, in private conversations with the pastor in hopes that he (most often "he") would respect their need to keep this information from others. But why trust this untrained counselor (few ministers get solid and formal training as therapists or counselors) who wasn't likely to be reprimanded if this confidence was broken? The pastor had the upper hand and could always spin the "facts" to his (usually "his") benefit.

"More of you, Lord, and less of me . . ." was a common mantra for the people in my church and for Christian folks elsewhere as well, but it had a special meaning for the minister whose job was to interpret and present the "Word of the Lord" and the teachings of the church. The preacher opened outlets for spiritual expression, orchestrated collective fellowship, and monitored the faithful.

Who could argue against the preacher and the Bible? This was particularly the case if the attack was made with passion, with words like "It's not me, brother; it's the Word that condemns you . . ." The trick was to couch such remarks in a "Hate the sin . . . love the sinner" approach. The rhetoric was really pointless because the distinction was rarely maintained. And what would maintaining this difference mean anyway? The targeted party was marginalized and labeled a sinner—our version of shunning.

I'd learn the fine art of this shunning, and my status as minister only enhanced the angst I could produce in others through a side comment or a well-placed and humbly presented piece of church gossip. Much of this gossip revolved around things like who was seen at which club; who was involved with whom; who was wearing a dress too short or too tight; which man must not have faith because he lost his job and started drinking; who seemed to be gay. Any such episode at my church or most of the churches with which I was (and am) familiar could generate a bad case of shunning combined with praying for (or preying on?) the troubled sinner.

Men showed emotion only in church, although they were to love and care for their families—and no one raised questions concerning the latent homoerotic nature of the male's relationship to the male savior. Nor was it mentioned that *black* men in my church (and churches like my church) prostrated themselves before images of a *white* Christ. Was there a hint of white supremacy in this move? This wasn't discussed. Loving and surrendering to this Christ emotionally and physically was okay—it was an act of manhood not to be duplicated elsewhere in life.

To be a black Christian man meant to be stern but fair and compassionate, heterosexual, family oriented, financially in charge (despite who made the money), properly dressed, and walking with an air of confidence and dignity premised on the condition of one's soul and one's status in the house of the Lord. All the guidelines were laid out in the Bible, codified in sermons and prayers, and celebrated by the church community on "Mother's Day," "Father's Day," "Children's Day" and so on. These named Sundays were special days for gender training in that they rewarded approved behavior and embarrassed those whose family situations didn't fit the religious-cultural model.

Years would pass before I was able to recognize the ridiculous nature of this thinking. Until then, I was just another kid learning to be sexist and homophobic—all in the name of God.

Accepting these cultural and social arrangements offered me a space of life meaning that served almost like armor. For a child going through all the typical childhood stuff, and within a family not always easy to negotiate, these arrangements provided a form of identity stability that seemed to stand the test of time. I'm not saying my family was reality show–ready, but it had its issues and there was something calming about fitting into church life and learning early what my role could be.

My life as a minister-in-training, as a preacher (to be) of the Gospel of Christ, was under way in a modest but highly visible fashion. I don't recall my mother raising any concerns about it, and I remember even less about my siblings and their response. My father would have been opposed but not involved enough to make a difference in my thinking.

There were no other children in my church playing the role I was playing. The others might be Christians who'd surrendered themselves to God, but they weren't going to have the relationship to the church or God I was to have. The boys might become righteous men and the girls, righteous women, yet they wouldn't be called Reverend or Pastor or Minister, like I would be someday. They would be loved by God but not "used" by God, and they wouldn't serve as God's spokesperson.

All this being said, at that point, mine wasn't an official position in the church's hierarchy. When Reverend Hudson took me up on my claim to ministry, there was nothing in the official administrative makeup fitting my responsibilities. There was no financial compensation of any kind and no job description to discuss with my parents. The position was an odd mutation—something between a lay reader and an assistant minister without the full responsibilities of either. I think of it as Reverend Hudson being creative, but it was too early to know if there was a distinction in my case between fascination with a profession and God's demand on a human life.

Reverend Hudson gave me responsibility for a good portion of the morning worship service, although I didn't preach. There was no manuscript preparation for me at this point. What would I talk about anyway? With few exceptions—illicit sins—the preacher was to pull from life experience marked by temptation and sins overcome, and from wisdom and insight expressed as the Bible is interpreted. My world was small and didn't contain much that could be of inspiration or importance to those beyond my years, who actually knew something about living in the world and of making decisions with consequences. There were family issues—parents on the verge of divorce, a brother who followed his own path that at times included rough living—none of which I could explore theologically with any depth and present through compelling narrative. My theology was simplistic and without much grounding in my own reading of scripture: Jesus is the "son of God"; he died for our sins; we go to hell if we don't accept him as savior . . . and God loves us so we go to church to express our love for God and God's rules. It was Sunday school–ish and peppered with "just because" pronouncements.

What I knew about the church and the Christian faith wasn't sufficient for sermons, but it was enough for other rituals associated with Sunday service. I gave morning prayers, prayed over the offerings, and lined the morning hymns.

There I was leading the congregation in morning songs. I read a verse and the congregation sang it. In addition to this, and more important, I also led the invitation to Christian discipleship on some occasions. After Hudson gave his sermon, I offered those present an opportunity to accept Jesus Christ as personal savior, or for those who were "saved" an opportunity to rededicate to a life defined by the Gospel of Christ. This might seem like a small thing, but it was the biggest of my obligations. Hudson wasn't much of a dynamic minister; he didn't "get the people going," and he didn't whoop—preach with strong gestures and movement—so there weren't many joining the church.

But even so, my words pronounced on the steps leading up to the pulpit were the point of entry and the first welcome to those accepting Christ. Thinking back, even this involvement on my part seems irresponsible, or maybe at least a marker of how little was at stake in the process of joining the church.

The church, although it has its forms of pressure and demands for conformity, is a voluntary organization. People could be as involved, or not, as they liked, and although the pastor could preach heaven or hell, there was no real evidence of either. So, members of the church and the target audience of the unsaved in the pews had to buy into the reality of the church's claims. They had to suspend disbelief and accept the religious claims of the minister. *Faith*.

For those of us in the church, there was nothing more important than salvation, and as a young man, it was quite a responsibility to call sinners to accountability and to encourage saints to continue the fight against sin and sinfulness. I was responsible for pointing out ultimate concerns—heaven and hell, eternal life or eternal damnation—that were embedded in the pastor's sermon. I didn't have a script for this invitation I'd extend, and I don't remember at all the words I used. However, I must not have offended people.

That Hudson kept me in the pulpit performing these responsibilities meant there weren't significant challenges from key members of the church (those giving good money and those who were part of the original membership) to my role. I sat in the pulpit with him. The childish games were over; I no longer sat in a pew where my mischief could go relatively undetected. I was in the pulpit, and my movements were exposed to dissection. I had to be careful, set an example for others—monitor my behavior.

This need to monitor what people thought they knew about me was a price I had to pay, but it came with appreciation and more authority as well as more visibility than one would expect a child to have in an adult world.

I enjoyed this status. Of course I did.

Chapter Five

CHURCH POLITICS

My minister-in-training role continued for the time Reverend Hudson remained with our church. However, ministers at smaller AME churches tend to move—and depending on their performance this could be a demotion or a promotion. I'm not certain which it was for Hudson, but with time he was gone.

At some point, I don't remember when, rumors begin to fly that we were getting a young minister from Philadelphia. He and his wife had spent time in Africa as missionaries—and he brought that missionary zeal, a theologized sense of black consciousness and pride, a commitment to community engagement, and a charismatic personality to his church in Philadelphia. The fact that he was a Harvard-trained preacher received mixed reviews: while some thought he might be conceited and might have "lost Jesus" in that godless place, others were impressed and considered him a reminder of the AME Church's rich history and glory. Some of the best of its ministerial giants had similarly prestigious degrees.

We'd heard good and bad things, but no one denied his reputation as a church builder and that's what we needed. We were a tight but small congregation needing to grow.

Things changed with Reverend Fred A. Lucas Jr. in the pulpit. He was young and dynamic, wearing an Afro, the fashion of the 1970s, and gold glasses. Young people identified with him and so they flocked to the church, old members who'd left over the years came back, and the curious came to check out the church. Sunday after Sunday, people came to hear this young guy preach without a manuscript. Lucas's sermons were energetic and full of references to current events and popular culture.

Lucas knew—perhaps Hudson or some of the members, maybe my mother, told him—that I had expressed a desire to be a preacher and that Hudson started that process by involving me in the order of service. Lucas did a bit of that as well, although I imagine he had to have his suspicions concerning why people would be so interested in this child preaching and why this young boy would be so willing to surrender childhood in order to preach. He'd ask me to do special readings from African American literature or to read scripture. I didn't open the doors of the church after the sermon anymore. He slowed my process down some and gave me opportunities to experience church work as a child.

I became one of the church's first acolytes responsible for carrying the flags to their place in the front of the sanctuary, lighting the candles on the altar, taking the offering plates to the altar, and leading the procession out of the sanctuary at the end of the service. We acolytes had our own dressing area in a side room near Lucas's office. We'd get to church a bit early, rush to that room, take off our jackets and put on the bright red cassock and the white covering. After looking at each other's shoes to make certain they were clean, we gathered our supplies and headed to the back of the church where we waited for the musicians to signal the start of the service.

We weren't ministers, and this role didn't involve a "calling" like being a preacher did. Still, we were proud to have been selected and asked to play this role. Reverend Lucas picked us and told us the importance of our tasks, and we were honored.

We handled our responsibilities as best we could, but we were children and we found ways to entertain ourselves—quiet conversations, trying to make each other laugh, falling asleep, playing with the hymnal. (I played around in this role more than I had while working as a minister-in-training with Hudson. The stakes weren't as high as an acolyte.) Sometimes our games went unnoticed, even though we were in the front of the church, but other times, Reverend Lucas caught us and gave us a look of annoyance and correction. We'd straighten up to keep him from being disappointed with us. Although we had fathers at home, Lucas was something of a big brother, father figure, and professional role model for us.

Image 7. The author on Easter Sunday, with his mother, father, and sister Linda.

My parents' relationship was just about over during the early phase of Lucas's work at Agape Church. And it's sad to say his thinking on the situation wasn't any more progressive than the typical black church response: "Lead your husband to Christ through your example, and avoid divorce because it isn't consistent with biblical teachings and the will of God . . . the Lord doesn't give us more than we can bear."

That was all fine for him to say. He didn't have to deal with the tensions in my home, the brazen misconduct on my father's part. Lucas could sit in the relative comfort of the parsonage after he gave spiritual advice to my mother, while we went back to 348 Florida Street to our messy family dynamics. My mother tried to follow his advice, but it finally reached a point where even she had to acknowledge the marriage couldn't be saved. They separated when I was about ten, and then divorced.

The day my father left the house for good was one of the best days of my life. I felt relief. I could sleep at night, worried only about my mother's health and without the added burden of having to sleep lightly in case my parents argued and I had to intervene.

I didn't have to worry about my mother in the same ways anymore. Looking out for her physical health was familiar and I could do that, but the other ways in which that marriage was destroying her were beyond my control, and prayer hadn't made a difference in her lot and my life. We could now depend on divorce court and not the altar, and that was a better arrangement.

My father didn't move far, just a few blocks away, with the new woman in his life. I was embarrassed by his new arrangement so close to me and in view of all my friends and neighbors, but I could work around that. I could spin a different narrative. Overall, I was so much happier.

Even the visits my mother forced me to make to my father's apartment located above a local bar I tolerated, as long as I could come back home to a house without him. I put up with the stupid questions from his new partner, the disrespectful comments made under her breath, and I overlooked his awkward efforts to connect with a son he didn't really know all that well.

Image 8. The author as a young child on Christmas Day, with brother Raymond, sister Joyce (in back), and sister Linda.

I thought about it as an hour or so disconnected from my life, kind of like holding my breath for a while knowing the discomfort was for a confined period of time. Whether justified or not, whether Christian or not, I didn't care. I was growing numb toward my father. I attended his funeral years later, but without much emotional attachment—just like attending services for an acquaintance or a distant relative. I'd lost my father long before his funeral, and I had no tears to shed for him.

My mother told me God would take care of us and would meet all our needs. Yet I knew she worried that—apart from my father's involvement in our financial affairs—I no longer had a male presence in my life. It's not as if I would have become a gangbanger or a drug dealer without my father's guidance. There was enough pressure from my family to keep me away from all that, and I really didn't have the stomach for the physical confrontation that both might require. My life wasn't a "Lifetime" movie, nothing quite that dramatic and formulaic. Yet there was more to it than going down the wrong path.

The gap, the lack of a male role model, was filled from time to time with the presence of my brother or my sister Linda's boyfriend (now husband). They were role models to some extent, but the person who took on that task most frequently was Reverend Lucas.

With Lucas, I had a sense of what it meant to be a man and, based on my vocational claims, also a sense of how to be a man of God. That was an important combination, and I looked to him for lessons on how to achieve it in ways that earned me the approval of my fellow church members. It was a matter of having a model of success within the church; what it meant to be a man and a man of God was another dimension of the guidance I needed.

I listened to how he talked, watched how he walked and dressed, and noted his actions. He was a man of distinction, and I was going to be a man of distinction as well—a preacher with a fine reputation and a successful church ministry. I wanted to be seen as a man of God, respected and valued; and in this way I would be like Fred Lucas.

Of course, this was the type of egoism permitted within my church setting: I want to be someone special and important . . . *for the glory of God*. It easily became a form of passive-aggressive behavior in that any selfish or self-serving wishes could be attributed to God, who was responsible—not the Christian, who actually delighted in the misfortune of another—for the consequences faced by those who denied a man of God what he wanted. God first, but a great *me* after God, and anyone who doesn't get in line with this vision is outside the will of God and subject to punishment. Damn, that's a good gig!

It wasn't long before Lucas revisited my calling to ministry. I don't remember all the details, but it involved more than the rather casual process I'd gone through with Hudson. I had to explain to him my calling and how I "knew" this was what God wanted for my life. I also had to do something similar with the church membership. Memory is faint, but it probably went something like this: Standing in front of the church with my Bible under my arm, I answered questions first from the leadership of the church and then from the presiding elder, the minister who supervised the congregations within the region of the Episcopal district of which my church was a part.

"Are you a Christian, Tony?"

"Yes."

"Have you accepted Jesus Christ as your personal savior?"

"Yes."

"And you have been baptized?" (In the AME Church we weren't pushed under the water like in Baptist churches; we had water sprinkled on our heads. This was meant to accomplish the same thing for a church unequipped with a baptismal pool.)

"Yes."

"Are you called to preach?"

"Yes."

"How do you know you are called to preach?"

"I feel it in my heart."

"Have you prayed about this?"

"Yes, I have."

"How do you know that feeling you have is the Lord calling you to preach?"

"I feel the leading of the Lord."

"Couldn't this be your family wanting you to preach?"

"I think it might make some of my family happy, but I believe it is the Lord."

"What is it you want to do with this calling?"

"I want to be a preacher and pastor a church."

"Aren't you very young for this?"

"I am young, but the Lord can use young people too."

"Do you want to be a minister in the AME Church, Tony?"

"Yes, I do."

"Do you feel ready and able to preach?"

"Yes, I think I am."

"What makes you feel ready at your young age?"

"Because I pray, I am born-again, and God can use anybody."

My answers had to be in line with what the presiding elder expected to hear. I must not have sounded too young or too unfocused or uncertain. My language must have been Christian and convincing enough because my last answer was met with a response something like this:

"Church, pray for this young man as he begins his ministry. Care for him and work with him."

It was over and I was relieved. I believed I was called, but the questioning in front of everyone was a difficult experience. I'd gone from an initial announcement of my desire to be a minister, wherein the subjective measuring stick of my *feeling* constituted enough to legitimate my call, to a situation in which I had to explain it all.

It has been a good number of years since those church meetings, and I can't remember the exact details. What I can remember and what my mother remembered put me at roughly twelve years of age when I reached this point of commitment and gained a different type of access to the pulpit. I'd reached the age of accountability, which is the time when I was fully responsible for my doings and thoughts, and that would be the right time to finally test my commitment to ministry. Even if I wasn't exactly twelve, I know I started preaching long before I could vote, or defend the country, or drive, or do any of the things associated with maturity and adulthood.

I had given evidence that I had more than a self-interested desire to be a preacher and to reap the benefits involved. I'd articulated my calling in a convincing way, and this entitled me to a "trial" sermon. Everything about my calling was real once I'd defended it to the faithful and had a date set for my trial sermon. It was a coming out of sorts, an introduction into a particular religious and social circle. It was the preaching community's equivalent of an initiation.

The trial sermon was just that—the first sermon given, a pulpit practicum. It was the final test of a person's calling demonstrated through performed ability. The criteria used to assess this ability to preach were subjective but typically had to do with the sermon bringing people to salvation or repentance for sins committed, or the preaching giving those gathered an indescribable sense that the Lord was present.

At least in theory it was possible for someone to be told after their trial sermon that there was no clear evidence of a calling on their life and that they would not go through the formal process leading to ordination. (My grandmother, when talking about preachers she'd encountered, described this type of situation as the person seeing "GPC" in the sky and assuming it meant "Go preach Christ," when it really meant "Go pick cotton.") I don't recall ever witnessing someone being turned way, even though there were some sermons given after which people whispered complaints and questions.

The trial sermon preacher typically was given the benefit of the doubt. Maybe there were nerves because it was the first sermon? Maybe the person was still learning how to be open to the inspiration of God in writing and delivering the sermon? Or, there was always the fallback position that God ultimately knows the human heart and will judge that person's calling. And if there isn't really a calling, God will expose that in God's perfect time.

This trial sermon was a foolproof process, as far as we were concerned. If the new preacher turned out at least halfway decent, the church claimed a new worker. If the new preacher turned out to be nothing but a problem, God was ultimately responsible for dealing with the situation.

My maternal grandparents, the Hargraves, were very proud that their grandson was going to be a preacher. There hadn't been one in the family for some decades. My grandfather was so proud that he gave me his personal Bible to use in preparation as well as on the day of my sermon. My grandmother reminded me that this was just the beginning, that if I was going to be a preacher, I was going to be a well-trained preacher. She said she wouldn't make use of the services of an attorney, who didn't have a JD degree, nor would she visit a doctor without an MD degree. In like manner, her grandson wasn't to be a "jackleg" (that is, untrained and questionable) minister. I'd have to be educated and, from my grandmother's perspective, do this thing right.

But that was a distant concern. I was only a preteen and about to preach a trial sermon before I could vote, serve in the military, or travel too far from home without permission or a chaperone. God could speak even by means of the "mouths of babes."

Initially my trial sermon was to take place during the week, as part of a midweek service, but Lucas changed it to a Sunday morning. This was a big deal—a strong statement of the importance of the event, and a bigger audience as a consequence. However, the sermon wasn't going to take place in the main sanctuary because it was being renovated; instead, it would take place downstairs in the fellowship hall set up to look like a church sanctuary.

There was good bit of buzz around the event—a young boy preaching a first sermon. People came because they were part of my church family and part of my biological family, others were supporters of those seeking to live out their calling, and still others made their way to my church out of curiosity: what could this child possibly say about the Word of God?

My mother reminded me that I would need to pray for God's guidance, but I'd also need to prepare a sermon after the Lord provided inspiration. I might need to fast in order to make certain I was open to this inspiration, but it was important that my sermon be more than my own thinking, my own opinions. Despite this prep work, Reverend Lucas—with a smile—reminded me that I should leave a page of my sermon blank for the Holy Spirit to speak through me. This was his way of reminding me I should not write a sermon that ruled out the possibility of God seizing the moment and doing something special through me. "Let the Lord have His way!" My time in the pulpit could not be all mapped out and fixed.

I needed to work on a sermon that told the people they could trust me to speak the will of God and to provide the faithful with a "good word" that would help them make it through another week. As the ministers would say, "More of you, Lord, and less of me." This is one of the catchphrases I'd need to employ. It was a stock phrase for preachers in the pulpit. And it was an important statement because it gave the congregation the sense that there was more than ego at work in the pulpit.

"May the words of my mouth and the meditation of my heart be acceptable in thy sight, my strength and my Redeemer" was another statement

meant to accomplish the same outcome. The words assured the congregation that the sermon was the result of inspiration and that it spoke to more
than the personal idiosyncrasies of the preacher. Although this happened more
often than people in the church would want to admit, the pretense was that
the sermon wouldn't simply be an opportunity for the minister to take slaps
at people without consequences.

I knew what was expected and what to avoid, but no one actually taught
me how to develop a sermon, how to connect daily occurrences with ageless
biblical truths. I'd heard plenty of sermons and understood the end product,
but how to reach that stage, how to develop something worth saying had not
been taught. I guess the assumptions were purity of intentions and a true
calling would open the preacher to the leading of the Lord, and God would
provide the vision and the words. Prayer, fasting (to control the mind), and a
"quiet spirit" waiting on a word from the Lord were the basic requirements.

Thinking back, it was all a bit haphazard. The sermon that confirmed and
shaped the theological sensibilities as well as the moral and ethical commitments of Christians gathered on a Sunday was going to be given by a child
without training, without expertise, without a clear sense of what life entails.
The sermon was as close as you could get to the meaning of God's presence for
human life; it marked an intimate connection between the Word of God and
human life exceeded only by the significance of communion.

But I hadn't even read the Bible cover to cover enough times to understand its nuances and embedded concerns and conflicts. I didn't own Bible
commentaries to help with this research; instead, the sermon would be a strict
product of my imagination. I would share opinions I'd heard others express,
all filtered through the limited grasp on life held by any person my age. I
didn't have a style of preaching to rely on. I didn't have experience as a public
speaker beyond what Hudson allowed me to do or the times I'd given special
readings when Lucas became pastor. I didn't have particular movements or
hand gestures that marked my way of preaching.

Lucas didn't stand in the pulpit and read to the people. And I wouldn't do
that either; I'd follow his lead and only use an outline—developing the basic
points and leaving the rest to the inspiration of God's Spirit. I'd use an outline,
but I wasn't certain how to do that: was it like writing an outline for one of

my school papers? The teacher checked my papers, but who would check this sermon outline? I couldn't ask my sister Joyce to read it over, couldn't ask my mother or grandparents. To do so might feel like I was questioning my calling, or that I didn't have the type of relationship with God or spiritual discernment preachers should be able to call upon whenever necessary. I'd have to figure out how to do this thing myself. After all, I was the one called, the one who was supposed to have the spiritual connection to God. Getting this sermon ready wasn't like getting a school assignment done. There were souls at stake, not just a grade.

I had been trained to believe that doubt was of the devil and that it had to be overcome through faith in the face of uncertainty and fear. It would be a mistake, I thought, to let anyone think I wasn't certain about my calling—particularly because my father had questions about it and I wouldn't do anything that might suggest he was right about my involvement in church (or anything else, for that matter).

I don't recall exactly how I prepared my trial sermon. I imagine I read the Bible and watched a lot of the *700 Club* for inspiration. I know I thought about it and tried to keep my mind open to inspiration. Finally something came to me, and I jotted down notes in preparation for that special Sunday morning. I thought about giving that inspired word and played it out in my mind. There would be lead-up activities—announcements, songs, prayers, and so on—then a sermonic hymn. As that song was sung, I would do what I saw other preachers do: kneel facing away from the audience and pray. I would stay in that position until the song was almost done. Then I would mount the pulpit and proclaim the Word of God.

I don't remember much about the time leading up to that Sunday. Did I behave differently in school? Did my classmates know? Did I interact with my siblings differently? I don't know. I do remember the excitement of my mother and the pride of my grandparents.

When that Sunday finally arrived, I put on my suit, my glasses, my shiny shoes, and I wore the facial expressions I assumed matched those of someone serious about his religion. We arrived early to church, and I made my way to the pastor's study with my grandfather's Bible in hand. I'd been in there before, but not like this—as the one giving the sermon. I was in the ministerial club and the others in the office treated me appropriately, calling me "Preacher" and making certain I was comfortable. I was getting a glimpse into the preservice ritual for ministers. I watched how they interacted, how they sat with their legs crossed showing their color-coordinated socks set against their shined shoes, and how their pressed suit pants were matched by a jacket and coordinated tie. I listened to how they spoke about their gifts and successes preaching to the people and how they "played the dozens" with each other. It was a more down-to-earth vibe than I'd expected. I assumed they would be serious, deep in thought, communing with God, and readying themselves for the awesome task of a Sunday service. Who knew this preparation process involved jokes and laughter—some pretty mundane things.

We stayed in the office a long time while things were set up downstairs in the makeshift sanctuary. And this gave me time to think. I wondered if people would come to hear me. If the church was pretty empty, what would that say about my ministry? Would it mean people didn't have confidence in my calling and my ability to preach "a good word"? I didn't want my nervousness and questions about people showing up to be evident, so I kept control of my facial expressions as I had learned to do.

When it was time to leave the office and head to the fellowship-hall-turned-sanctuary, I walked behind the other ministers. We entered as the music played and people sang the opening selection. The seats were full with family, friends, and lots of people I didn't recognize. We went through the order of service: songs, prayers, scripture reading (based on the scripture from which I would preach), announcements, greetings, and offerings. It was just as I had imagined it. Right before I was to preach, Lucas made some remarks about my calling, assuring people that the anointing of the Lord was on me. It was a kind of endorsement from the minister-in-charge.

Once he finished, the sermonic selection was played, the people sang and then took their seats. I walked to the wooden pulpit—all the time looking out at smiling faces and kind eyes. I stood as tall as I could and gripped the sides of the pulpit for comfort and stability.

I said an opening prayer, ending it with the words preachers say to center Christ and remove themselves: "Let the words of my mouth and the meditation of my heart be acceptable in thy sight, my strength and my redeemer."

I was aware of my voice like never before. It wasn't deep and booming; there wasn't even the sound of a young man maturing, with voice cracking. I sounded like a kid trying to sound like a tough and capable preacher.

I read the scripture for my sermon and looked intensely at those gathered, just as I'd seen other preachers do.

After a quick look at my outline, I started preaching.

Moving from a measured and even tone to a more impassioned and energetic tone with arms moving and weight shifting from one side to the other, I cautioned people about their sins and their need for salvation. I told women to dress with respect for God and self; I told men to value women, and I cautioned both men and women to avoid improper relationships.

I spoke against hypocrisy—live what you claim—and peppered it with promises of redemption for those who honestly and earnestly reached out to God. I told them about God's love, the death and resurrection of Christ, and Christ's second coming when we least expected it.

They had to be ready, every day watching for the Lord's return! We must live knowing Christ is on his way back to us.

What I proposed was puritanical and, in retrospect, rather amusing commentary coming from a kid who couldn't leave the house after dark and who had no interest in most of the sins described. I was too young to be serious about girls, not old enough to buy my own clothes, and without independence. But this didn't stop the congregation from responding with traditional church callbacks to each comment I made: "Amen!" "Preach!" "Say that . . . well . . ." This speaking back was the mark of a good sermon; the people got involved and felt what was being said. The words rang true to them, and they encouraged me to continue.

I paused as I finished my sermon and looked with as much earnestness as I could muster. Then I opened the doors of the church and invited people to come to God.

I told the congregation that God was a forgiving God, and that sins could be surrendered to God in exchange for salvation and righteousness. I invited those who wanted to forsake their old lives of sin to come to the front, right below the pulpit. I urged those who'd already accepted Christ but were not living in accordance with that commitment to come forward as well.

This was the real test of my sermon, the best sign that I was in fact called to preach: Would anyone be moved by my sermon to come forward?

The congregation sang the "invitation to Christian discipleship" hymn, and before the song was done people came forward to give their lives to Jesus the Christ and to become members of the church. I don't know what eventually happened to them, but at that point I was certain they were saved from a painful eternity without God and were now on the righteous path because of my preaching.

Because people came forward, I had proven myself something of a spiritual equal to other preachers who had brought people to Christ. My sermon may not have been as complex, may have lacked the same rich description and the same refinement of performance as others, but it had done the trick; it had accomplished what the sermon is meant to accomplish. People congratulated me for letting "God use you in a powerful way."

After that Sunday, I had a different role. I was on my way to becoming a licensed preacher, authorized by the presiding elder and the AME Church he represented to preach on behalf of Agape Church. And Lucas allowed me to preach at some of the midweek services as one of his "children in ministry."

My process for preparing sermons was simple: read the Bible, meditate, watch religious television programming, and wait for an idea to hit me. When it did, I called it divine inspiration. Once in the pulpit, I would present a problem or concern as the topic for the day. I'd follow that with thoughts on how the scriptural passage connected to my sermon spoke to the particular problem. Then I would outline what the scripture teaches us to do regarding the problem or issue. At the end I would invite people to get saved and join the church.

It was the same process each time, always the same formula. The words flowed, and I figured if I did my part—pray, try to live in a way consistent with the demands of my faith, and study God's Word—God would be responsible for the rest.

When I wasn't in the pulpit, Lucas exposed me to the networking dimensions of ministry, including meeting other ministers, attending community-organizing meetings, dinners, and other church-related activities. This was to give me a fuller sense of what the preacher's life involved beyond the Sunday service. Invitations to preach at other churches came in, and I could accept with the permission of the pastor . . . and my mother.

She traveled with me when I preached at other churches, and for as long as I lived in her house I was not allowed to accept payment—a "love offering" of cash—in exchange for preaching. She said that all my needs were met and there was no reason for me to receive a fee for doing what God had called me to do. The gospel wasn't for sale, but other ministers—most ministers—received some financial "thank you" for their preaching. I didn't really understand why I couldn't receive compensation for preaching. Where was that in the Bible? Isn't a "work man worthy of his hire," as the Bible says? If so, why couldn't I accept money, particularly when things were often financially tight for us? It wasn't as if we were rich; a bit of money would help a lot. The child support my father paid didn't cover very much and this could have been a way for me to contribute to the meeting of family expenses. Despite this logic, my mother said no, and that was the end of it. So I'd preach, refuse the offering, and leave.

Depending on what was happening at my home church, we might head there after I preached elsewhere. When we did that, church mothers and the pastor would ask me if I "preached." They weren't concerned with the mere fact that I'd been in the pulpit. Theirs was a question about the quality of my sermon. Did it have an impact? Did people get saved? Did the spirit of God descend and people dance in the spirit, or did the spirit take me over, and did I whoop? Had I preached with passion?

In addition to asking these questions, Reverend Lucas would touch my shirt. If it was wet from sweat, it meant I must have let the Lord work through me, that I'd preached with energy. (Few of the churches had air conditioning during the summer, but that cause of perspiration was never factored in when testing me.) There were physical signs of God's presence, and how much a preacher sweated during a sermon was one of them. The body was pushed, heated up, in order to give God full run and control over the flesh and the mind of the preacher. However, if my shirt was dry, or if there were no other signs that I had worked up a sweat, I'd probably just "lectured," which wasn't a good thing.

Lecturing. There was in the accusation of lecturing a negative association between book learning and no spiritual "burning"—too much thinking and not enough of God's Spirit freely working. Lecturing meant the preacher remained in control rather than surrendering to the leading of God. Lecturing centered on the preacher's words, and thinking as opposed to divine inspiration and communication. With a lecture from the pulpit, the preacher remained the focus as opposed to being merely a vessel used by God to give the people what they need. It was assumed there was no room for the Holy Spirit in a lecture (passed off as a sermon).

When done "right," worship service was understood as something of a filling station, with the sermon providing the fuel necessary to move through another week until Christians could recharge again. This is how I'd been taught to think about worship. And because this was popular thinking in my church, ministers were approached with deference, even when they were as young and inexperienced as I was. We ate first. We had a pitcher of fresh water in the pulpit, along with mints to keep our throats ready to speak. There were members of the staff who helped us put on our robes and take them off, who stored and cleaned our robes, and who provided rides wherever the Lord's work took us.

Successful ministers had something of a sheltered and privileged life, and members of the church took pride in providing it. In exchange, the minister was to provide inspired and inspiring sermons, provide good counsel, and avoid publicly embarrassing the church. Yet there were complexities: how to push people to be better without offending and driving them away? Should controversial issues be brought up in a sermon? Preachers had to set standards. But how to preach these standards when the minister might be just as guilty of ongoing sin as anyone?

In my denomination, unlike in Baptist churches, ministers weren't dismissed by a vote of the church. But powerful people in many local churches could complain to the bishop, hint they might leave and take their money with them, and the bishop might be "inspired" to move the minister from one AME church to another. So no minister could feel completely at ease, despite all the perks and benefits that went along with a calling to preach. Even ministers like me who didn't pastor had to wonder what each sermon might mean for their reputation and their ability to one day secure the pastorate of a prominent (and well-paying) church. It was never too early in a preacher's career to think about such issues and begin to plan and prepare.

Our *Book of Discipline* provided the nuts and bolts of church obligations, authority, and responsibilities, but as a young minister I didn't read it. I'm not certain most ministers did. Instead we drew from the Bible (although I'm not certain we actually read it with any type of discipline), a little from the main creedal points of the church (repeated during each service), personal encounters with God, and a vague theology developed informally. This was the case in particular for ministers and church members not in seminary or divinity school and not prone to read theological texts beyond Sunday school materials or what was recommended loosely during Bible study meetings.

Seminary was encouraged, and many of the more prominent ministers, such as my pastor, had the professional degree for ministry: the Master of Divinity degree. However, the *Book of Discipline* wasn't clear on this, and it hadn't been updated to reflect things such as the educational level of parishioners that demanded an equally well-trained clergy. And so the seminary question was addressed haphazardly, depending on the particular presiding elder and bishop in place and their personal educational background and inclinations. However, educational requirements could be sidestepped, particularly if the preacher in question had impressive sermonic skills.

Because I was so young, formal theological training wasn't a possibility. Instead, prior to college, I attended the ministerial institute offered by my denomination. It was founded during a period when admission to seminaries and other theological schools was restricted by race. In addition, it provided some type of training to those for whom seminary was beyond financial reach. Finally, it meant those coming into ministry late in life received some training.

The classes met on Saturdays, and senior ministers from local churches taught them. Much of what took place, as I remember, involved these senior pastors talking about their exploits and successes in the pulpit and sharing anecdotes about the life of a preacher dealing with difficult parishioners. Despite what actually took place, the idea was to study church polity using the *Book of Discipline*, some theology, church administration, as well as the basic points of the church's official rituals and practices.

After each set of courses, students were tested and either promoted to the next round of courses or required to do additional work before moving on.

Going through the institute process was a requirement but of no more use than any other pro forma activity requiring no thought—just a willingness to go through the motions.

We dressed like it was Sunday, sat in the room, listened to the senior minister talk about anything on his mind, got our assignments . . . maybe did the reading, and waited for the next meeting. Easy. At the end of several years taking these courses, ministers were to have a "working" knowledge of the church and their duties sufficient to pastor a (small) church or mission.

Like those around me, my personal theology tended to be evangelical in tone and conservative in outlook but with some sense of racism as a wrong to fight. It was tough on personal sin while having at least a soft awareness of institutional structures of discrimination. Sin was personal with a hint of collective injustice gathered from a superficial understanding of the civil rights movement. However, both forms of sin—personal and structural—were handled ultimately through appeal to Christ and spiritual gymnastics.

I believed in a literal heaven and a literal hell. The former was reserved only for those who'd committed themselves to Christ and who lived in accordance with that commitment. I didn't believe that members of other religions were going to heaven; in fact, I didn't give much thought to them at all beyond the occasional expression of Christianity's superiority and the recognition in the Bible that Christ would not return until all had an opportunity to hear the Gospel. I thought this was sufficient when combined with the biblical proclamation that nature and all of life pointed to the reality of God and, by extension, the truth of the teachings of Christ. So, everyone had a chance to be saved, if they desired. Those who didn't deserved hell. Period.

My sense of hell wasn't very sophisticated; there was nothing of Dante in it. Deeply painful, full of misery, flames that never stopped licking the bodies of the condemned, with the righteous looking over a cosmic railing basking in their righteousness. It was a kind of eternal "I told you so."

A variety of things could result in damnation. For example, I understood sex was wrong outside of marriage, and the body—its wants and desires—was at best suspect because it served to pull us away from God. Its urges ran contrary to the will of God; this much we learned from Adam and Eve. Talk of Adam and Eve should have raised a variety of issues for me concerning how the earth was populated. Further, if these two and their children were the first people, who was it that Cain, after killing Abel, feared?

Although my mother purchased for me a book on evolution I still own, and evolutionary thought was a given within my public school education, I didn't give it much consideration. Based on the truth of the Bible, I assumed that God created all that is. I wasn't preoccupied with the time frame for God's acts of creation. Seven days or not wasn't the point. That God created all things and controlled all aspects of life *was* the point.

I believed in the Trinity, and that God the Father, God the Son, and God the Holy Ghost were real and each played a role in the life of the saved. The Father provided salvation and punishment; the Son made this salvation possible and offered a role model for human life; and the Holy Spirit provided special gifts and abilities, such as speaking in tongues, the ability to heal, dancing in the spirit (the Holy Dance), and so on. Everyone wanted one or more of these gifts, but in my church we didn't fixate on them like they did in the Pentecostal churches nearby.

I believed all we needed to know in order to live properly was contained in the Bible—the Word of God, inspired by God and recorded by humans. There might appear to be contradictions and inconsistencies in the text, but I gave little attention to these because even they were subject to the power of God. Oppression so blatantly outlined and celebrated in the Bible didn't mean much to me. Sexism, homophobia, and so on weren't critiqued in my sermons. These forms of injustice worked their way into my church life and thinking and seemed natural because they were found in scripture and affirmed in my denomination's policies. The Bible and the church, as two primary sources of authority, made these forms of oppression somewhat natural and right.

I understood the relationship between the church and struggle against injustice, but this revolved around racism. And my community work hinged on evangelizing sinners and bringing them to Christ. The saved got to keep their sexist and homophobic opinions as long as they learned to express them through the language of scripture and the grammar of church tradition—"the Bible says it and I believe it."

The very appearance of evil was a problem. I was to avoid all appearances of evil and most activities that couldn't be conducted within the church fell into this category. Secular music could be a problem in that it glorified the "world," yet I still listened to it and enjoyed it. Television also projected a world with morals and ethics we believed to be different than those advanced by Christ, but I continued to watch as much television as I could. We were in the world but not of it, and if you had strong faith you could even flirt with things of the world—as long as those things were somehow subjected to God's authority. There was slippage, a porous boundary between "good" and "evil." How to negotiate this boundary wasn't always clear and typically involved contradictions and a bit of hypocrisy covered by appeals to scripture and personal revelation.

On occasion I cursed, had lots of inappropriate thoughts and desires, and in so many other ways presented myself as human. This put me in good company with biblical figures and contemporary heroes of the church. But as long as I acknowledged my shortcomings and asked sincerely for God to forgive me, everything was okay. (It wasn't as if we could ask for forgiveness only a certain number of times; there was no way to max out as long as forgiveness was achieved before death.) And, as a minister, there was no need to share this information with anyone or to ask anyone for guidance or assistance.

I could keep my stuff between God and me, and no one had to be the wiser about it. The ability to discipline my facial expressions and to confine my conversation was already in place. I'd learned those skills as part of life in my family, and they came in handy in the church. For the faithful, this made me kind of stoic, a contemplative man of God who was so sensitive to the spiritual world that it affected his interactions in the material world. "He's serious," they noted, convinced I was a man of God with little time for superficial things. They were wrong: it was a response to my life and my insecurities. It was an effort to protect myself, to hold the pieces of me together as best I could. I wasn't certain how I would have expressed all of this even if I could have. For me, spiritual growth wasn't necessarily matched with social maturity.

My relationship to the world was complex, and that's the way the Christian faith, as I experienced it, preferred the arrangement to be. I saw the world as attractive but hostile to my beliefs and determined to keep me from Christ with all sorts of temptation. At its best, the world was useful, yet things of the world were not to be trusted and were to be approached prayerfully with the "full armor of the Lord"—prayer, faith, righteousness, and so on—in place to deflect attempts by the "enemy" to turn me from Christ. Worldly joys and pleasures covered deeper struggles of powers and principalities at war, and I had to be careful not to become a casualty of war. I had to guard against eternal damnation.

My theology—my way of thinking about and talking about God and God's relationship to humans and all life—nurtured a cruel take on humanity and the world of which we are a part. In a passive-aggressive way it sanctioned violence through its "insider" versus "outsider" group configurations. Those who abided by the same theology and held to the same faith commitments were part of the insider group and were God's people deserving of all good things. However, the outsider group was not part of the community of those God loves, and any abuse they received was deserved because they did not know Jesus the Christ in the free pardon of their sins. In a twisted way, we even prayed for their misfortune so that their suffering could be used to break them and bring them to repentance and salvation. I, like those around me, believed it was necessary to destroy pride and any sense of self-determination held by the unsaved before they could realize their need for divine compassion, grace, and forgiveness.

Even when saved there was always the threat of slippage, of failure to follow through on the exact will of God. There were psychological consequences to this perpetual fear that something done or said might disappoint God. My fear, a dimension of the morality and ethics connected to my theology and my faith, was expressed in a variety of ways, including a recurring dream.

I often had dreams about my mother and her health, and my inability to do anything to make her healthy and keep her alive. But this recurring dream was about me and my salvation, not about my mother. Others were in it, but they were vague outlines and didn't figure prominently in the action. It went like this: I was on a bus driven by Satan—a large figure with horns, piercing eyes, and the legs of an ox—and I was desperately trying to get off the bus, screaming and crying that I believed in and worshipped God. Satan laughed and continued to drive. As the bus would stop to pick up others, I would try my best to get out the door, but my body wouldn't move. My faith wasn't enough. My faith didn't prevent me from riding with Satan down the wrong path.

In hindsight it is a ridiculously silly dream, but as a child it felt all too real and telling: if I didn't fight against my desires and wishes (what could a child really wish or desire that would be so troubling?) I would not make it to heaven. But I had been trained in church to look for opposition, for signs of Satan and the unsaved trying to test me and hamper my spiritual growth.

Every day I was haunted at some point by the thought that I might not be good enough, that I might not represent the faith well. I hoped that others felt this way so that I could believe it was just part of the faith. I wanted this anxiety to be shared so that I could make it normal, so that I could tame it by making it a communal infliction. I feared not being "good" enough, and so my initial gut response was to hope no one felt good enough. Still, this didn't prevent me from worrying that it was just me and that other Christians had stronger faith and were much closer to God than I was or would ever be. I had questions about my faith and my calling—and I fought these doubts as best I could.

I would tell myself that biblical greats had their moments of doubt and they overcame them. Yet it seemed different in my case. I'd have to keep at it, push through it, hoping for good results. Catch my breath and keep at it, desperately wanting to hold to the belief that God, in God's wisdom, would work things out for me and through me. God had to be in me and on my side.

It's an odd way to select and develop a career and life based on the wishes of an invisible force called "God." But what's more, it's a force without any physical evidence known only through a collection of stories. There were other invisible forces that peppered my childhood—Santa Clause, the Easter Bunny, the Tooth Fairy, and so on—but they had defined bodies and tasks for only a limited period of time and with clear criteria that determined how I should behave. But God's desires seemed contradictory and often mean-spirited, even for someone who was now on the inside of the tradition. Unlike those others, God had an organization—the Christian Church—charged with employing and caring for God's employees.

In retrospect, this Church doesn't seem to have much more accountability than this God seems to have for humans. It does what it wants and chalks everything up to its relationship with this God. This international organization has limited accountability to the US government—no property taxes paid and no substantial obligation to indicate how money is used, and the government offers it more money to carry out these mysterious tasks. Its clergy pays limited taxes and real major benefits come their way—and seems to do what it wants when it wants and how it wants. Now that's a "gangsta" move!

For the most part people inside this organization go along with its program. No need for guns to enforce its will, although some of the more bizarre versions of this Church go "old school" and use weapons and physical warfare to bring about what they sense as God's will. But most, like my church, didn't go this route. The threat of hell and the rewards of heaven typically are persuasive enough to get significant numbers of people in line. In fact, the teachings, what I was growing to understand and learning to preach, played to human greed and insecurities.

There was abuse in the church family—gossip, deception, jealousy, discrimination, justification of injustice . . . the list continues. All this nastiness was covered and sanctioned through the theology I was learning. My "God-talk," or talk about God, was about safeguarding God's reputation even at the expense of the humans I loved and the world in which we lived. Protecting God from critique and challenge was more important than anything else.

God was the major reason for everything, the source of everything, and if God were "still on the throne," all would be well. If God fell to human questioning, the entire structure of my faith would collapse because it was all premised on creative power and unlimited knowledge owned by God. With God's demise would come the destruction of everything else God held together. "Try me and know that I am God": that line from scripture was God's posturing. And this posturing could only be pushed so far before the system imploded.

The only option I could see at that stage of my thinking was to protect God and, by means of that act, assume other things would fall into place. That was my hope and that was my faith.

I would come to appreciate these sticking points only later in life, but as a child preacher my safety zone was the church. Being a part of it provided support and the tools necessary to live, even when this living was a struggle against my own desires and wishes.

The price for this safety was emotional commitment, physical labor on behalf of the church, and, of course, the tithe—10 percent of one's income given to the church. This "voluntary" giving came with a return: give your 10 percent, and God will give you even more in both spiritual and material riches. It was a better return than any other investment opportunity available to us. "Seek ye first the Kingdom of God," the mandate goes, "and all other things shall be added unto you."

The fee was worth it to me, although I had little personal resources. I did have time and a commitment to service, and I was determined to give these things to God. Evangelical missions on the streets of Buffalo, trying to lead the lost—pimps, prostitutes, drug addicts, and the like—to Christ was part of what I did. Preaching in churches and praying for the saved and the unsaved was my unpaid work. And I did all this, as a child, for the glory of God.

Chapter Six

CAN YOU SAY, "BOB JONES"?

The city of Buffalo consolidated the "special progress" programs for "gifted students" into City Honors School, moving me from my school across town to this new one located a few blocks from my home.

City Honors School was the best the city of Buffalo had to offer in the form of public education, but being secular, it presented a difficulty for someone with my type of theology and training as a minister.

I felt like I was on a college campus, or at least what I'd heard about college campuses and what I'd experienced with my mother when a small child. Students were free to leave campus when we weren't in classes, and classes covered a liberal arts model of education with each taught by one of the best teachers in the city. This school was in the heart of the city, not far from downtown and very close to a group of colleges. The building itself wasn't memorable, but it had a different energy and an openness that was unusual. It was a hardcore academic environment, and this was important. I understood it was a big deal being there, but I was also concerned with my religious development—and that dimension of my life was of no interest to my teachers.

Spiritual health and intellectual advancement could—must—be compatible and in line with the same goals and objectives. As far as I was concerned, the town and gown, the church and the classroom didn't need to be in conflict, as long as the welfare of the soul took precedence. "All things work together for the good of those who love the Lord and are called according to his purpose" was a biblical line I used to interpret life's various arrangements—including schooling.

I viewed school to some degree through the biblical assumption that "we wrestle not against flesh and blood, but against principalities and powers . . ." I was in the physical world, but there were unseen forces attempting to manipulate human behavior, and these forces wanted to prevent me from living a righteous life. These demonic forces were everywhere, even the halls of City Honors.

I interpreted my interactions with other students and faculty in this way. Even the slightest offense would be seen as an effort to derail my Christian life and ministry. A student bumps me in the hallway, and I first think: Was that because he knows I'm a Christian? Someone spills something on me—did they do that on purpose, to test my faith? Were these small events or markers of this cosmic battle and my role in it as a called and committed Christian? It was easy for me to see everything as a test of my faith, as an effort by the unsaved to take away my joy. Though attending City Honors affirmed my gifted status, this wasn't a long-term arrangement.

Because I was committed to evangelical ministry, education meant attending a school with the same religious commitments and theological perspectives. I wanted to be with the like-minded, to receive my education within the context of a shared commitment to Christ. My mother agreed that I should be in an environment where there was no conflict between my need for education and my need for spiritual growth. So I left that public school and enrolled in West Seneca Christian School. It was an extremely conservative (and at times, racist) Baptist institution at which I was the first African American student. Most students at West Seneca went on to continue their "education" at institutions like Bob Jones University. Enough said, right?

My mother also saw this new school, some distance from my house, as an opportunity to demonstrate her Christian virtue at my expense. Never wanting to turn me against my father but rather to raise me in line with the scriptural mandate that children recognize their relationship to their parents, she made me spend time with him. This meant getting up really early in the morning to ride with him (and sometimes the new woman in his life) to South Buffalo where he'd drop me at a bus stop and continue on his way to work. It was a rough area, even early in the morning before the sun came up. I'd always been told that South Buffalo didn't really appreciate black people, and that was why we didn't spend much time there—just a quick trip to the meat market and then home. I grew up believing there was hostility toward people like me in that area of the city and that there was always the threat of violence should I venture there.

Fortunately, the worst I encountered were racist remarks shouted from passing cars and whispered comments from other kids making their way to the bus stop as the sun came up. I wasn't physically threatened, and I credited God with protecting me from those who might want to do me harm. As a servant of God—a preacher—I was set apart and God placed a shield of protection around me, I thought, despite my mother placing me in a bad predicament. Her effort to prove her righteousness put me at risk, but I understood that God—being a good God—turned even that misguided spirituality on my mother's part into a situation affirming and glorifying the power and grace of God. Whatever the case, I made it to school each day without major incident and made it back home in one piece after basketball or soccer practice and games.

Founded in the early 1970s and tied to First Baptist Church of West Seneca, this small school was about the business of providing education that reinforced the conservative and Bible-based teachings of the Southern Baptist denomination. While the state required certain educational outcomes, the Word of God was the basis of all true knowledge for this school, and it alone contained the blueprint for all human thought and activity. The world was the enemy, but the world also was a missionary field, and West Seneca Christian students were being trained to bring this world to Christ regardless of the career path chosen.

Most of the teachers were young and energetic, trained at conservative religious schools, and they understood their work at this school as a form of mission. The older teachers were just as committed to the students. Both groups of teachers understood us to be at a delicate and vulnerable age—when hormones rage, curiosity rules, and the risk of sin is profound. But even the teachers had to be monitored. The contract they signed limited their own social outlets and required membership at the sponsoring church. They shared theology, religious commitments and rituals; they shared a common social outlook.

All the usual elements were included in the list of things the teachers (and other church members) were to avoid—secular music (although we students listened to it), secular films (watched by students and discussed during lunch), and premarital sex. They also pledged to honor scripture and to recognize religious authority. These teachers were exposed to "Big Brother" and the ever-watchful church family meant to save them from themselves and the evils humans are so inclined to embrace.

These were Christians of a certain hue who, as far as I could tell, had limited exposure to people from my area of the city. They were the type who only ventured into the city for sporting events or to lead services at the Salvation Army downtown, where they'd hold the hungry and homeless hostage to their theology and missions work: Listen to the sermon *and then* you can eat. It didn't seem to me that they had much practical experience with treating as equals people who looked like me—an African American.

It was some time after my arrival that I found out there had been a meeting at the school to discuss how to incorporate me into their "community." I can only imagine this involved a conversation concerning how to maintain their doctrinal beliefs and be as "PC" as possible. I imagine some of them had viewed *Roots* and wanted to be understanding and sensitive.

Some regulations related to students made it clear they weren't developed with someone like me in mind. Males couldn't have hair below their collars, but that wasn't a challenge for me with my Afro. They had no regulations for the size and shape of an Afro because they'd never encountered one outside television programs or sporting events. There was a regulation concerning sideburns not going below the middle of the ear, and I tested this rule on numerous occasions but rarely was I called on it. They weren't always certain how to correct the black student without fear I'd take it the wrong way. We couldn't wear jeans, but no one knew what to do about my bright-colored khakis worn on some occasions, let alone other fashion statements that were associated more with my neighborhood than the suburbs. How could I not take a little of the city with me? My clothes often weren't consistent with their aesthetic, but they weren't outside the formal rules. Christians come in different cultural styles and social categories, and the people at this school were confronted with the truth of this statement.

I had to take placement exams, and this meant most of my classes weren't with my tenth-grade classmates. I had a good number of my classes with higher grades because of my education at City Honors. This, I'm certain, created a bit of sociocultural dissonance for people at the school. The stories they'd heard and believed about the city suggested that African Americans lived a degraded existence and shouldn't best them intellectually—at sports, maybe, but education? . . . No. I didn't speak like the stereotypical depictions of African Americans in the "urban jungle" suggested we spoke. I wasn't a crude caricature in line with sitcom-warped and cartoonish presentations of African American identity. I could put a sentence together; I didn't sell drugs; I didn't have a bunch of babies; my family wasn't on public assistance; and so on. This made me something of an oddity on that campus.

Who is that black guy from the inner city?

On my first day everyone was anxious to make me feel welcomed, to demonstrate that his or her Christian world was big enough to include an African American. They, however, were obviously curious about this Christian from the city: how did I survive the dangers of urban living? Why was I joining them in the suburbs? What kind of church did I attend?

Whites visited my church on occasion, and there were a few "urban pioneers" in the neighborhood, but for the most part "Sunday is the most segregated day of the week" was a true statement for me. We worshipped differently. We assumed white Christians didn't have much energy during worship service. Of course, the television evangelists we followed did, but they weren't like most white Christians. The Holy Spirit and the gifts of the spirit were important at my church now that Reverend Lucas was in place. People spoke in tongues. People danced in the spirit. There were prophecies given. Tears were shed, and people shouted their happiness in praise of God.

I was fairly certain whites didn't do all of this, and they certainly didn't stay in church as long as we did. Two and three hours for church service weren't unusual for us, followed by an afternoon service, and sometimes an evening service at a different church. Sunday was packed with activities. High-energy worship was encouraged, and some people in the church would whisper, "Anything dead should be buried." By that they meant quiet worship wasn't pleasing to the Lord. Our joy, our spirituality should be expressed loudly, with excitement and passion. If we could be loud and uninhibited while watching sports, I'd been told more than once, didn't the Lord deserve as much energy for the gift of salvation? The cultural differences I assumed to be in place during worship had to surface during the school day.

Everything we were to learn in school spoke in some fashion to the majesty and glory of God. This wasn't so much the case with advanced science classes because they were taught by a member of the State University of New York at Buffalo faculty, who belonged to the church but brought his posture toward scientific investigation to his work at our little school. The real difficulty was the Bible class meant to create theological conformity in an odd way: we spent most of our time memorizing Bible verses. This take on the Bible included allegiance to its more troubled and troubling dimensions as well. Being a feeder school for institutions like Bob Jones University meant it embraced a compatible theology of race that privileged whiteness and sought to control the interaction between races. The university admitted blacks by the time I was in high school, but the school's ban on interracial relationships, for example, remained in place until long after I was out of school—out of graduate school and working as a full professor at a major university, in fact.

Some of the leadership of the church and school were graduates of Bob Jones University, and students from the university made an annual pilgrimage to our school. There was a special assembly during which they sang and talked to us about Jesus and the university. They weren't explicit about the racial politics of the institution, but there was no need for that. Just me being there—and, for a while, with a few others—didn't threaten their perception of the "in group" of which they were a part. Bob Jones University, from my vantage point, provided theological cover for a culture of racism. With a smile and a song, representatives of this perspective—to differing degrees—at my school felt religiously obligated and authorized to see me as different and to invest that difference with real meaning.

As a courtesy, my school tried to downplay the more offensive dimensions of this thinking, but "nigger" wasn't an unknown term at West Seneca Christian School or at similar institutions we encountered during basketball camps or other outings. My blackness was okay within limits, as long as I didn't challenge social and cultural regulations. After all, I imagine some of them reasoned my salvation should result in acceptance of biblical perceptions of racial difference. We are all God's children, but that didn't mean we should "mingle" in all conceivable ways. Being friends was fine, but as my limited contact with the girls at that school made clear, nothing more. "My parents aren't racist, but . . ." was the mantra; yet I was in no hurry to take any of the girls to my neighborhood either.

I'd get invited to skating parties and other afterschool events, and sometimes I'd go. There was nothing unusual about these activities other than that they served to reinforce my "two worlds" situation: I had friends and responsibilities back home in my neighborhood and I had a life at school. But the two never connected.

There were a few white students who lived closer to me than to the school, and with time we'd ride the bus together—a few of the girls in the morning and one of the guys after soccer and basketball practice. The travel gave us something in common. We didn't live in the suburbs; we were city kids— from different sections of the city with different social and cultural assumptions but still from the city.

The racial politics of faith jibed with normative social politics at the school. My church was on the other side of the race issue, but, like my school, it theologized its cultural perspective on the meaning and function of race. The whites at my school had questions concerning the place of blackness in God's design for human life, and we had questions at my church concerning whiteness. At the church associated with my school, the stained glass window aesthetically represented their sense of themselves and race, whereas the images displayed around my church looked nothing like us, and we sang about being washed as white as snow as a metaphor for righteousness.

Whiteness seemed to trump blackness in religion and in social relationships. If blacks could fit without disrupting the system, fine, but this toleration was based on the superior bestowing something on the inferior. In this case, allowing me into their world on a temporary basis, with only the occasional slip of the tongue or odd look to indicate the type of xenophobia their theology actually encouraged.

For those at my school, their race and its importance was embedded in the signs and symbols of the faith. For me, my race was beautiful despite the lack of presence in the symbols and signs of the faith. Sure, people in my neighborhood were "color-struck," and internalized oppression meant we talked about "good hair," "pretty eyes," and so on. Yet we understood ourselves to be beautiful, drawn in the image of God regardless of sociocultural and political pronouncements to the contrary. This was our faith, a bit schizophrenic, but ours nonetheless.

My neighborhood and my church remained my primary locations for self-understanding and identity formation. They were the places where I became me. At home and in church I was special—not because of my race, but because of my calling.

"Home"—made up of these two—was my centering something. This was despite the fact that between school and athletics I typically didn't get home until dinnertime, then there was homework (including the memorization of Bible passages), some television, and sleep before starting it all over again. But the week was also peppered with church activities, like Bible study, and the weekends contained church starting on Saturday. I did my chores, had choir rehearsal or some other church activity, and Saturday evenings I hung out with my church friends—video games, movies, skating, shopping . . . dating. Sunday was church, and Monday back to school.

The school made me hyper-visible, a cultural and theological spectacle, which made being there a delicate balancing act. I had to maintain my self-regard as a child of God and as an African American in an antiblack society, and I needed to do this without calling too much additional attention to myself.

Neither the perspective of my teachers nor the training of my church really prepared me to address this dilemma. It couldn't be handled through a spiritualizing of life and the dismissal of the material world. The answer I had to this problem didn't satisfy when I wasn't in the classroom or the church sanctuary.

Some of my religious sensibilities were shifting. I had a growing awareness of the odd ability of the deeply religious to consider themselves righteous and spiritually advanced while also being xenophobic, sexist, racist, and so on.

There were cracks in the theological armor of the people at my school. These shortcomings were made evident when they had to interact with me in personal ways, when they made an effort to "include" me as one of them. At times, their remarks were racist. This wasn't the "spit at you, burn a cross on your lawn" type of racism. It was more passive than that, and it was couched in what they thought to be compliments: "Tony . . . you're not like the others . . ." was said with a smile as their sign of comfort with me. The identity of these others was uncertain; they were a nondescript group formed of fear and assumptions concerning African Americans.

Image 9. Graduation from West Seneca Christian School.

Through an odd and twisted logic, they thought they were doing me a favor through this verbal rescue. They were saying, "Tony, you are like us and we can keep you around without fear. Don't get too close, but you aren't what we typically envision when we think about blacks. Don't ask too much of us and don't push this kindness in ways that challenge our cultural assumptions." In a word, they wanted me to be their version of a safe black.

This situation posed a dilemma: Do I take visible offense and respond, and what would I gain in letting people have it when they made these types of remarks? Or do I let it slide off my back and save my more aggressive comments for the retelling of what happened once I got home? Over the course of my three years at that school, I moved between these possible responses. It was always a matter of balancing religion and race.

My circumstances were made more complex by the hormonal changes taking place in my body. These teen years were understood as dangerous years when sexual urges, experimentation with drugs due to peer pressure, disrespect for parents and family played out in a quest for independence and personhood that led away from Christ. Anything beyond a desire for a relationship with God or appropriate relationships with others in the family of God easily led to poor conduct that harmed the individual, did damage to the reputation and standing of the Christian community, and denied God.

"Yield not to temptation, for yielding is sin. Each victory will help you some other to win." These are words from a song we sang often in church, and for some it was all the answer they needed to respond to the questions posed by their changing bodies and the things those bodies want. I wanted it to be that easy, but for me it wasn't.

I had a Bible and religious creeds and doctrines, but they did not explain how to be a teenager in the late 1970s and early 1980s. This was particularly the case with the taboo subject of sex. To say I wasn't given a healthy way of addressing sexual urges is an understatement. I dated at the church and flirted with dating at school—the race issue was always present and splashed cold social and theological water on any strong interests in the girls there. The fact that I was pretty shy didn't help in either context. Still, I did all right in the dating world. But whether a group date or one-on-one, "courting" had to take place in a way that brought glory to God. Elders in the church thought they handled the situation by telling us that dates always involved at least three because Jesus was present with us. Jesus as a third wheel was supposed to hamper our desires because we shouldn't do anything we would be uncomfortable doing in front of Jesus.

Jesus, the savior of the world, had a penis (typically not depicted in the images), but his sexual ethics—what he did with that penis, who received pleasure by means of it, and how Jesus received pleasure as a result of it—was never spoken of. To even think about Jesus having sex with men or women was construed as sinful because it meant reducing the God/man to a human controlled by a sex organ. Doing so was to point away from the ministry of the Christ and instead to replace his saving work with the yearnings of a physical body. To think about Jesus's body parts in that way might force a reconsideration of Jesus's relationship with Mary Magdalene or, in a more challenging twist, the disciple whom he loved. This thinking wasn't orthodox, and it lent itself to an array of theological problems, particularly because I'd been taught that Jesus the Christ was tempted like all humans but without sin. Of course, sex outside the context of marriage was sin as far as I was concerned. Sex wasn't restricted to procreation, but it was a pleasure only appropriate within the context of strong commitment represented by marriage.

I wish there'd been a way around that theological conclusion, but at that point in my life there wasn't. According to what I'd been led to believe, even masturbation was a problem. Typically it was the topic never discussed, but we assumed it was not a good thing because it involved fantasies, and even these thoughts of sex were sinful and could lead in the direction of physical activity.

Direct lessons regarding personal conduct we mistakenly got from figures such as the Apostle Paul and other early followers of Christ. We maintained their perception of history as coming to an end through Christ's return, and this Second Coming meant we should give priority to preparation for the Rapture and bracket the needs of the body. Responding to these needs could result in us being left behind when Christ came back. The goal was perfection, a life completely devoted to God. But achieving that was hard at best.

Those teen years were difficult for young people in my church, and even more so for me because I was also a preacher. Fasting, prayer, and other forms of control and discipline became a way to get a hold on my body and what my body wanted. These activities were all ritualized and written into the codes of our faith communities.

Modest attire was used to draw attention away from the body and toward heaven. My church wasn't as strict as some Pentecostal churches. Women could wear makeup and pants—but not too tight. Men were to be modest in their dress as well. This meant no tight pants, no suits that looked as if they might be worn by a pimp. We were not to carry ourselves in a way that made bodies anything other than vessels for the will of God. However, the most effective prophylactic against improper conduct was the Holy Spirit.

The comforter and guide that Jesus the Christ promised when, after the resurrection and contact with his disciplines, he ascended to heaven.

My denomination and my local church didn't demand people be filled with the Holy Spirit as evidenced by particular manifestations like speaking in tongues, a language one hadn't studied or wasn't raised speaking. Yet we believed those who were saved could receive the Holy Spirit, and we believed the Holy Spirit provided strength necessary to resist all forms of temptation. It's no wonder my encounter(s) with the Holy Spirit seemed to have a direct relationship to my growing into adulthood, my maturation and push through puberty.

The foggiest dimension of my religious life, the portion of it that in hindsight I am least able to understand and unpack with any strong degree of certainty involves what I perceived as my relationship with the Holy Spirit.

Spirit possession by the Holy Spirit was the gold standard of spiritual development. Prophecy, healings, and other happenings only available because of the Holy Spirit working through a person were highly sought. And, as a preacher in training, one who wanted to be embraced as special, I wanted all these gifts.

The Bible provided some guidance, but the tests for determining if someone actually had the Holy Spirit were spotty within my church. If we'd had more stringent demands that the person speak in tongues and have it interpreted by another person present, this situation might have been easier to manage, but we didn't. The person didn't have to dance in the spirit, didn't have to heal others, and didn't have to overcome poison and other traumas that would typically destroy human bodies. Instead, the person only had to believe and communicate that he or she had the Holy Spirit. Disproving the claim was difficult and would be based on circumstantial evidence and subjective judgment. Official church doctrine couldn't trump these more informal conversations and tests of authenticity.

I don't remember exactly when I began claiming the Holy Spirit. I was saved and following the will of God as best I could, and at some point I spoke in tongues and danced in the spirit. I had what church people called a prayer language and public moments of "speaking in tongues." With the first, it was a private language used in private prayer. I had control over it, and it was used to prevent Satan from interfering with my prayers. Evil forces couldn't understand a Christian's prayer language, so the requests went directly to God. I believed God responded much faster to the request made in a prayer language than to prayers in one's normal language. It was appropriate anytime it was needed, and it marked me as a prayer "warrior." The prayer language was for the individual. Speaking in tongues publicly, within worship service, was for the benefit of the community. So it was understood within my church that whatever was said had to be interpreted publicly, or the person speaking had only created confusion. No one wanted to be accused of creating turmoil because it came with a stigma difficult to live down. Maybe they're faking it, and that wasn't pleasing to God and it wasn't edifying to the church. And it only took one episode like that for a person's sanctification to be brought into question.

I don't remember the first time I spoke in tongues for the edification of the congregation. It wasn't something I willed. Speaking in tongues during a service happened when God saw fit for it to take place. I could feel it coming on, like a seizure, but I couldn't do anything about it. For as long as the public speaking in tongues went on, I was controlled by another force, although I was aware of what was taking place and could hear the words coming from me.

One minute I was praying at the altar of the church, and the next thing I knew, I was speaking out loud in an odd-sounding language. It almost felt as if I was outside and above my own body, watching myself speak this language—head thrown back, eyes closed, tears forming, arms outstretched, back straight, and muscles taut.

This language flowing from me was met initially with silence as the church waited for the Spirit of God to touch another and give them the interpretation. It could be a few minutes, but my words were countered by something in English—a warning against wrongdoing, encouragement for someone suffering or going through trials and tribulations, or a reprimand for those not living as they should. What people did with this rather standard information given in a fantastic manner is uncertain, but the experience meant God was present in my church in a special way. God was working through the congregation and its leadership, bringing strength and truth to the people of God in the last days before Christ's return. To the extent I played a role in this, I was believed to be anointed, a prophet among preachers.

Speaking in tongues, dancing in the spirit, and other manifestations of the Holy Spirit could take place during any gathering—a few of the "saints" present for intense prayer over a particularly pressing issue or an official service. Any time the faithful gathered and the situation demanded it, we believed the Holy Spirit could manifest. However, one of the more intense moments for the work of the Holy Spirit was the revival service. These meetings were meant to have the same energy and impact as the "Great Awakenings" that shook the religious foundations of first the North American colonies and then the United States—bringing people to Jesus and influencing the socio-political vision of a nation through an evangelical theology of change.

Think of these revival gatherings at my church as tune-ups, opportunities for the faithful to energize and boost their spirituality as well as a chance to bring sinners to Christ. These services were led by prominent and highly skilled ministers or evangelists who had a reputation for fiery sermons and fantastic performances with sinners saved and the born-again strengthened in their faith. My church held these revivals regularly, and, while we often invited preachers from outside the city, we also made use of local "talent." The reality of competing faith claims in my community (e.g., Nation of Islam and Spiritualism) made the revivals even more important because we were at war, trying to bring people to the true faith—the only faith that could provide salvation. In order to accomplish this, we had to be spiritually strong and focused.

I didn't complain about going to church every evening for roughly a week when it was revival time. God, we believed, would reward the sacrifice; if nothing else, it meant seeing my friends when I normally wouldn't until the weekend. Most of these revivals had limited reach and didn't linger in the collective memory of my church. We'd talk about the great work the Lord did that week, but the conversation quickly shifted. But one revival changed this pattern.

I don't remember exactly when it took place, although I know I was a student at West Seneca Christian School at the time.

The services had gone as they usually did. Some of the faithful went forward after the preaching and rededicated themselves to the Lord. Others went to the altar, prayed for themselves and others, and the tears flowed. Some spoke in tongues, others danced in the spirit, but these were sporadic episodes that I typically watched from something of a distance. That is, until the last night of the revival when I went to the altar to pray.

I don't know how long I'd been at the altar, but at one point I felt a hot flash and had this urgent need to get to my feet. Something was happening, and it made me uncomfortable. I felt as if forces were fighting over me and I was struggling not to surrender, to keep my senses about me, and to keep control of my body. Later, one of the church mothers who was praying with me said I told her something about the Lord wanting me to dance.

The next thing I knew, that hot flash was replaced by voices in my head and I was on my feet dancing—moving up and down, bouncing in place—with people gathered around me in a circle. I was talking to individuals there, giving them messages about their needs and how those needs should be addressed, reprimanding some and blessing others. And then another member of the church appearing possessed came toward me with arms outstretched. Although controlled by those around me and unsuccessful, he was trying to get me to stop moving, to stop talking, to surrender and be quiet. For us, this was a battle between God and evil forces played out in our small church, through two young people. Someone who'd left the circle and moved to the back of the church later reported that he saw spiritual fire surrounding me, as if cosmic power was emanating from me. In addition to this energy coming from me, he claimed to see spiritual forces moving around the altar area of the church.

I danced and spoke to people for hours, until morning.

When we finally went home, I had a hard time sleeping. I thought I heard voices—a spiritual conversation between forces about me, each making some claim for me.

In thinking back, there are a variety of ways in which this can be explained, but back then it was a clear sign for me of God moving in our midst—manifesting power by impinging on our material lives. I assumed this is how it must have felt for the disciples on the day of Pentecost, when the Spirit of God first descended and changed them forever.

Barbara Lucas, Fred Lucas's wife and one of the ministers-in-training, and some of the other leaders of the church held a debriefing session with us a few days later. It was an opportunity to come to grips with what had taken place. I told what I felt and experienced, and those in the circle remembered the evening from their perspectives. We were encouraged not to assume that the other young man was evil or that what had taken place indicated any permanent stain on him or a permanent blessing on me.

"God could use anyone" is what Barbara Lucas told us.

The takeaway was a greater sensitivity to the unseen forces working in our world that try to manipulate or guide us. I became much more alert and began to measure everything by the battle of spiritual forces.

This revival experience and the theology around it encouraged me to look through this world, behind its material arrangements, to the real happenings and the forces of power that orchestrated them. This physical world became the playground for spiritual forces battling about ancient frictions and competing claims. Each action in the world deemed unacceptable by those in my church could be associated with particular demonic forces. So it was easy for me to assume that misdeeds or bad conversations were the result of demonic influence. It was the demon of alcoholism affecting people, or the demon of greed, or the demon of sexual perversion, and the list went on.

While we named a variety of demons, we didn't speak much about divine forces other than the Trinity, although we believed in angels and assumed God dispatched them to be of assistance to us. Still, I was more likely to credit the intervention of Christ or the Holy Spirit than to assume the archangel Gabriel, or some other divine messenger, was responsible for the good occurring in my life.

With all of this invisible spiritual activity occurring around us, humans had to pick sides—either work with God to bring about God's will or be in line with Satan and his forces of destruction and damnation. I picked the former, and as a preacher of the gospel I was committed to getting others on the same track. This was serious business, and it was a lot of responsibility for a teenager. And despite what Barbara Lucas said about God using anyone, based on this revival, I wasn't just another person claiming a call to ministry who might be able to preach okay. Not only was I a young preacher with potential, I was also a prophet—one with a special connection to God through whom God worked in fantastic ways.

Word spread about what had happened that weekday evening. And that buzz gave me an enhanced status within an elite circle—the community of preachers—because I had access to spiritual gifts not all possessed. I got preaching opportunities and people wanted me to duplicate that revival experience. I never encountered again anything quite like it, but that didn't stop people from wanting it and assuming that if God used me like that once, God could do it again.

That evening of dancing in the spirit and prophecy meant a new dimension to my ministry. In addition to saving souls and calling sinners to repentance, I was also called upon to cast out demons.

It wasn't a regular part of my activities, but it happened on occasion. At times this took place in homes, particularly if the demons were known to be especially prone to offensive statements and acts. But the more common location was the church altar. In either place the demon confronted would act out by making a person jerk around violently, speak disturbing things in a different voice—normally a lower voice—or strike out physically at the people trying to hold the possessed person relatively still.

Only the strongest Christians at my church participated in exorcisms because of the dangers involved. Weak Christians stood a chance of having the demon or demons enter them. My job was to stay strong and make certain I was covered, symbolically, with the blood of Jesus to prevent the demon(s) from attacking and possessing me: "I cover myself with the blood of Jesus and Satan can't penetrate it. I plead the blood of Jesus!" All others around would do the same in order to prevent the demon, once cast out, from entering them.

These demons fought long and with strength you wouldn't expect from the particular people possessed. Young women fought with the power of men, children with the power of adults. It wasn't superhuman power like that of comic book superheroes, but it was more power than a frail human should have in them. The possessed person would struggle and push against us—one body possessed against a rotating crew of prayer warriors and deeply spiritual and gifted believers.

We had a sense of the type of demon by what it did and said through the person. For us, this was the process of "trying a spirit." We would name the demon in a confident voice. "I command you demon of drug abuse to leave this person. I command you in the name of Jesus!" And others on the team would respond with affirmations. "Yes, Lord! The devil can't withstand the power of the Lord!"

Someone might touch the person with the Bible. The demon would react by throwing the possessed person around, trying to move away, trying to get loose, and cursing those gathered. We would continue to pray to God for assistance and continue to demand that the demon leave and return to the pit of hell. Whether due to some type of sin or by explicit invitation, I believed the power of God was the greater force and it could subdue and control any expression of evil power.

The process of exorcism—what we simply referred to as casting out demons—might take minutes or hours depending on the strength of that particular demon or demons and the spiritual power represented by those gathered. We'd keep at it until the demon was forced to leave the person.

If the person did not forsake his or her sinful activities or in some other way invited possession again, the demon would return with greater force. Getting the evil spirits out a second time would be much more difficult. We also believed that some invited these demons to take possession in exchange for worldly goods or evil powers. These invited demons could be cast out, but it was hard work. They would scream that they were there by invitation, and the struggle was more energetic because of the invitation.

Were those possessed really experiencing some sort of psychic break, some sort of chemical imbalance, or treatable medical condition? I didn't know, but back then even if the problem could be identified that way, I might still have assumed evil forces as the ultimate cause of psychological problems. And this was despite the fact that I was well aware of medicine and medical illness based on my mother's condition.

Her condition, however, was never understood in my church as a result of demonic influence manifest as physical illness. She was a prayer warrior, a saint, a leader of the church, and her condition was simply a physical limitation she could overcome through faith and spiritual power. Her actions within the church and her private life as expression of faith put a quick end to any thought that demons controlled her. If anything, my mother's illness was viewed as a test from God or as an external attack from demons that couldn't get inside her. She was kind of like Job from the biblical book by the same name—whose body was afflicted by Satan (with permission from God), but whose soul remained pure and committed to God.

Because my mother was a pillar of the church, to call her spirituality into question would have been to undermine and interrogate the connection to God of all those within the church. If Sister Pinn isn't in line with God's will and she's doing all this work for the church and the Kingdom of God, are any of us really saved? What distinguishes my mother's works from our works, her prayers from our prayers, the fruit of her activities from the outcomes we expect from our faith-filled commitments? If she isn't righteous, who is, and how do we know? It was our spin on John Calvin's dilemma: who is saved and how do we know? We just didn't take it as far as he did—no predestination and no double predestination for us.

There was grace and mercy, and some things were only known to the mind of God and embraced through faith. This was vital because the hierarchy and spiritual assumptions of the church couldn't be toppled. Period.

Life's struggles and traumas were the result of slippage in our faith, or they were a test from God, or a challenge from the devil. Whichever of these possibilities were true, I, and others in my church, knew God was not at fault. Not in a fundamentally problematic sense, anyway. Even when a test from God, the tribulation was righteous punishment for wrongdoing, or it was a temporary condition that would allow great gain: "No cross, no crown."

My theology and ethics, our rituals and spiritual relationships were dependent on the righteousness and purity of God. If that went away, the religious system would crumble: preserve my perception of God at all cost, even our own welfare. Nothing was to pull us away from this stance, not even the loss of loved ones.

The loss of a loved one. I was aware of death through my mother's illness, but I had to deal with my grandfather's death as a minister of the gospel. And this was a very different situation.

During my grandfather's illness, my mother and I left our home on Florida Street and moved in with my grandparents. When I wasn't in school or at the church for some reason, I took care of him. I washed him and changed the adult diapers he was forced to wear. I fed him and monitored him. He was a proud man and didn't like his grandchild doing this for him. It reversed roles and pushed against his standing as a strong, self-made man who took care of his family and made a way in the world. Now he was fragile, thin, and in need of a teenager's assistance. My grandmother worried that I would resent them because of this labor, but that wasn't the case. I didn't mind. I loved them both and wanted to honor them.

There wasn't much I could do for my mother and her health, but I could care for her father. Being needed simply fed my sense of ministry and special status: I, not my cousins or others, was doing this for my grandfather.

There were tense times when he resisted any assistance and threatened to handle me if I didn't leave him alone. He didn't have the strength to put up much of a fight, so I was able to care for him in accordance with the instructions I'd received from my mother.

As he got closer to death and less aggressive about his independence, resistance turned to soft pleading. He didn't want to eat, to be cleaned. He'd look into my eyes, his eyes cloudy and moist, and ask me to just let him die. He was tired and he wanted life to end.

"Tony . . . just let me die; let me go home."

This was hard to hear, but I responded as I thought a good Christian and minister should.

"Grandpa, you can't go until God takes you. Until then, I'll take care of you."

I don't know if he found this comforting. I doubt it, but he resisted only with his words near the end. "Tony . . . just let me die." His condition again required hospitalization.

One day I was helping my grandmother get ready to visit him in the hospital. It took time because of her leg brace and her severe arthritis. And as preparations to leave the house moved along slowly, she had a feeling that we needed to get there quickly, but before we could get out the door the phone rang. It was a call from the hospital to say that my grandfather had passed away. Some years after that, when I was in graduate school, my grandmother would die, and I went home to attend her funeral. I didn't just attend my grandfather's funeral, however, I preached his funeral sermon, at his home church in Lackawanna. It was what he wanted—his minister grandson to send him off with a sermon. I'd have his Bible again.

People around me wondered if I could handle it or whether the task would be too much for a teenager who'd been Ashley Hargrave's caregiver during the last phase of his life. I imagine others wondered if I had the spiritual strength and maturity to do this particular job.

My grandmother had no doubts, my mother had no doubts, and if members of my extended family had concerns, they didn't express them to the person they'd called "preacher" or "professor" for years at this point.

There were a lot of family members around as we grieved, food always at my grandmother's house provided by family friends who wanted to give their condolences and ease the burden by making certain that the family of Ashley Hargrave at least didn't have to worry about food. I could only partake in these activities with family and friends in a limited way. I had a eulogy to prepare.

My mother reminded me that I'd need to depend on the Lord for the proper words to say, and from time to time she'd ask me if I had "a word to share." This was an inquiry into whether my sermon was ready.

I went about my days, and I'd read the Bible, prayed and waited for inspiration to come. Eventually it did, while I was in my bedroom back home on Florida Street. I think I was playing video games on the small television in my room when the general theme hit me.

My sermon was about different types of grief and mourning. On the day of the funeral, after the limousine dropped us at the church, I went to the study with the other ministers. I put on the black robe my Uncle Joe purchased for me so that I'd have the right look for the service.

When it was time to begin, we mounted the pulpit. I don't remember the songs that were sung or the scripture passages that were read, but I remember the sun coming through the windows overlooking the pulpit. So beautiful and serene, like in the movies.

I remember the look of my grandfather in the coffin—all his strength removed, the color drained from him, and the vitality of his life replaced by this still object.

I prayed kneeling, facing away from the congregation. I stood, went to the pulpit, and started.

I reminded them about my grandfather, his strength, his forthrightness, his pride, and his faith. I told them about grief and mourning that was the

consequence of regret; about mourning that was the result of selfishness—
wanting people around despite the pain and suffering they encounter because
it is easier for us. I moved on to mourning that has to do with the guilt that
accompanies the death of someone we've not treated properly and now have no
opportunity to make it right. Finally, I told them about true mourning based
on a deep love and respect, and I reminded them that this righteous mourning
has to give way to joy when we recognize that someone right with Christ has
been freed from the flesh and its sufferings.

I kept my composure and made my points. It wasn't until the end of my
sermon, when I said something to the effect of "Ashley Hargrave, I won't say
good-bye . . . I'll say I'll see you in a little while" that I broke down. As soon
as I returned to my chair in the pulpit, I turned, went down on my knees and
cried. My grandfather was gone.

I cried as people in the church—friends and family—shouted their joy for
the life of Ashley Hargrave.

During the meal provided by the church, people came to me and told me
they enjoyed the sermon. "I knew you could preach, but I didn't know you could
preach like that!" They thought my grandfather would be proud and pleased; my
mother and my grandmother were. Others gave me a hug and smiled, or they
shook my hand. Some said nothing and did nothing, and that was fine with me.

I don't know that preaching my grandfather's eulogy gave me any new
insights into my calling, although I remember it as important, if not transfor-
mative. If nothing else, it was a reminder of a few important lessons. It told me
that depending on God would result in good things and that being a minister
of the gospel involved performing some difficult tasks. These tasks revolved
around my home and church, and I tried to keep a distinction between those
spaces and my school.

I didn't share the details of my spiritual experiences or ministerial status
with people at my high school. In this sense, my life was compartmentalized.
Not along spiritual and secular lines, but based on cultural distinctions. The
more energetic dimensions of my spirituality were kept clear of the white
evangelicalism that marked my school.

I didn't think they would understand, and I was a teenager—maybe a
prophet, sure—and I wanted to avoid ridicule. I was already different and I

didn't need an added marker of not being like them. So I'd let them believe our religious experiences were similar if not identical, just in different cultural contexts.

They knew I wanted to be a preacher, but there was no reason I could think of to let them know that I preached, spoke in tongues, and danced in the spirit. I didn't want to believe that I kept this information from them because I was ashamed of it. Being ashamed of my gifts would have been a spiritual crime, and if I was ashamed of Jesus the Christ before humans, he would be ashamed of me before God. The consequences for this were too great, and so I tried to convince myself that it had nothing to do with being embarrassed. It was simply that at school they wouldn't understand and to explain would be to cast pearls before swine, so to speak. This was a delicate balance—culturally, socially, and spiritually.

In school I wanted to blend in without losing myself. In church I wanted to maintain differences and, in the process, remain humble by acknowledging status and spiritual gifts, but always deflecting personal merit by attributing all good things to God.

Chapter Seven

NEW YORK, NEW YORK!

My responsibilities at the church increased. I was given a ministerial assignment as a youth minister, and each Sunday I received my particular task for worship service—reading scripture, leading prayers, and so on. It all seems rather random now. Did Reverend Lucas pray over these assignments, try to coordinate our talents with these tasks, or did he simply think: "Tony is young, let him work with young people." Or, "Okay, someone has to lead prayer today. There's Tony, let him do it"? Were these responsibilities too minor, a bit trivial, without big consequences if they don't go well?

Whatever Lucas's thinking, the pressure to perform could be subtle at times, but it was always present. Whether or not the tasks were actually significant didn't wipe out the fact that we were responsible for them. If we slipped or failed in some way, it was on us, *not* on God. Our sense that God was righteous, all-powerful, all-knowing, merciful, and compassionate meant blame didn't really stick to God. The characteristics we associated with God were like spiritual Teflon centuries in the making. Our problems and shortcomings slipped off God time and time again and caused God no substantial damage to reputation.

We'd have to fight any doubt that this wasn't the case because doubt easily led to a preacher backsliding or, in less graphic cases, to experiencing a reduction in faith that induced loss of spiritual power made evident through ineffective sermons and unanswered prayers. Any preacher on our staff guilty of this would lose face, but it would also implicate Fred Lucas and bring "shame on the name of the Lord." The preaching moment held the greatest threat if people didn't come to Christ, but every dimension of our performance as ministers held a bit of this concern.

Lucas was training us, but it was also clear to all of us that people came to the church to hear and see him—not us. The bishop took notice of his success at Agape. The membership had grown significantly. Lucas did major repair work on the church, and managing that debt through community giving was a symbol of his success. Community engagement was at a high level with people in the city aware of the church and providing good public relations and buzz about our activities. Lucas's ministry gave us political recognition, and the church became one of the "must visit" locations for any politician seeking office and wanting African American votes.

He was "golden"—a rising star within a denomination that had more to offer elite ministers than a church in Buffalo, New York. He needed new opportunities to further develop as a minister.

Within the AME Church, ministers are appointed to a pastorate for one year at a time, and this appointment is renewed—or not—by the bishop of the particular district. The assignment for each minister, announced at the annual conference each year, is supposed to be the result of deep meditation, prayer, and a mysterious process of discernment. However, everyone knew there were pragmatic and political motivations behind the movement of ministers.

At times, churches complained to their bishop about their pastor, and it was clear that if he (or she) was returned, people would leave and take their money with them. In other cases, churches urged the bishop to return the minister. With this position there was also a subtle threat revolving around membership and money. In still other cases, the minister's particular talents were needed elsewhere—to manage or grow a congregation, for instance.

Our bishop was in a position to recognize Lucas's accomplishments through assignment to a high-profile and highly distinguished pulpit. During one of our ministerial staff meetings, Lucas told us that he was moving to Bridge Street AWME Church in Brooklyn, New York. He told us who the next minister would be, and it came as no surprise because Lucas had brought him to preach at Agape some time ago so we'd get a sense of him. The new minister was nice, energetic, and a good preacher, but he wasn't Lucas. Moreover, the transition couldn't have been easy for him, given that this would be the second time he'd followed Lucas to a church.

We didn't know what Bridge Street thought about Lucas, and it didn't matter. We weren't happy about this transition. Lucas was our pastor, my "father in ministry," and it seemed that just as the church was hitting its stride, the bishop was taking him away. We understood that this was a good opportunity for him, one that would make the most of his gifts and talents. But it still felt like we were being punished. Our hard work and faith were rewarded with the loss of the minister who'd provided the vision and leadership that had gotten us to this good place. Nurture and trust a minister, work hard to live out the minister's vision, and that minister might be taken and given to another congregation.

Bridge Street was an old and established congregation with a strong sense of identity and a prime place in the denomination. Agape Church's history stemmed back to the 1960s, but Bridge Street claimed to have been organized in 1766, incorporated in 1818, and affiliated with the AME Church as of 1820—only a few years after the denomination was founded. This gave it a legacy that most other churches in the denomination couldn't claim. The "W" in its title (AWME) stands for "Wesleyan," which indicates its deep connection to the very origins of Methodism in North America due to its founding by Thomas Webb (as a mixed congregation) who'd been brought into the faith by John Wesley himself.

The church was (and still is) located in Brooklyn's Bedford-Stuyvesant neighborhood, at that time an economically troubled area with a high percentage of people of African descent. Bridge Street was a marker of economic and political difference in the community because of its relative financial stability, its connections, and its legacy as the oldest ongoing black church in Brooklyn. It was the type of church politicians flocked to, and it had among its membership an impressive number of important city figures, including well-positioned attorneys, business leaders, and a host of others representing the middle class and the upper-middle class. But there were also those in the congregation who struggled economically and who didn't have the social and political pull necessary to get ahead. These members relied on their affiliation with the historic church for sociocultural capital.

People sat in those pews at Bridge Street for a host of reasons—deep spiritual need, social capital, networking, cultural outlet, and so on—and ministers had to be sensitive to this reality in order to be successful. Some assumed that only seasoned—older and experienced—ministers had the capacity to walk this fine line.

Lucas was young for that pulpit, and this fact had to get Bridge Street's attention. What could this young minister bring to this established church? How many others, perhaps more refined, had been overlooked in the process to get him to Bridge Street? Would he fit in, and could he transition from the loose and less historic story of Agape Church to the more refined story of Bridge Street Church?

As Lucas and his family were preparing for his transition, I was preparing for the next phase of my education.

High school was coming to an end, and I was applying to college—only secular universities outside Buffalo. Remarks made in passing along with looks on faces at my high school made it clear they were concerned about my spiritual well-being and perhaps had questions about the depth of my commitment to God. I was opening myself to being in the world and of the world, a dangerous move with eternal consequences that shouldn't be taken lightly.

Many of my teachers believed there was nothing a secular institution could provide a Christian that would be of much use—not in the long run anyway. To combine a proper education with spiritual growth required experiencing higher education at a religious—meaning evangelical—institution. If I really believed the Bible, if I really belonged to Christ, how could I even think about attending a school that didn't recognize Christ as King? Why not Bob Jones University, or Cedarville College, or even Gordon College, all conservative Christian institutions where my soul would be safe from contamination?

I didn't see it that way, and my church didn't preach that perspective on higher education. In fact, almost all the young people at my church who attended college went to secular institutions. We were taught to believe we carried Christ in us, and we didn't need to attend a Christ-centered institution in order to value the Bible and abide by the teachings of our faith. We could be "in the world, *but* not of it." This balance required that we be "prayed up."

With the Lucas family moving to New York, the decision to go to Columbia

University was easy on an intellectual level. After all, it was a great school with a tremendous reputation, and it put me in the same city as the Lucases. However, it was difficult emotionally. With my father gone, I had become my mother's confidant. Her health always concerned me, but with the divorce of my parents I also felt a growing responsibility for her emotional well-being. She shared her concerns and worries with me and confided her financial challenges as well. I was a young boy and then a teenager who had to play the role of an adult. I wanted to be my age, but between the loss of childhood coming with my calling into ministry and my mother's need for someone to talk with, I had to mature. At times it was a burden, and there were moments when I resented hearing what should have been information for adults only. Even in these moments, however, my ministerial impulse came into play and covered my animosity.

Leaving for New York was an opportunity to be a teenager, to live without some of the emotional responsibilities I shouldered in Buffalo. This thought of space and time away from these commitments was always followed by another thought: who would be there for my mother? I wanted her to be okay emotionally, financially, and physically. I comforted myself with the belief that my sister Joyce would be there and that my prayers and phone calls would cover the distance between visits. And so I was off to "The City."

I had an instant connection to New York. I loved the energy, the diversity; the idea of living in Harlem was big for me. I knew Columbia would challenge me. There were so many ways in which the demand for conformity at West Seneca Christian had put me at a disadvantage and trained me away from asking questions, making statements, and speaking my mind. College would involve a very different way of learning.

West Seneca Christian had warped my critical thinking skills and replaced them with a habit of conforming and responding to challenges and questions with scripture and blind faith. A properly stated passage of scripture in high school was better than a well-reasoned argument using only secular sources. Those secular materials were taught, and to that extent they were important, but they were superseded by the trans-historical reality of scriptural truths.

This next phase of my life would mean a new synergy between education and ministry that wasn't possible in Buffalo. In fact, even if Reverend Lucas and his family had remained at Agape, I would have needed to leave Buffalo. There was nothing about that city, apart from my home, that inspired me. I loved my friends, but most of them lacked ambition. They limped along expecting little from life, and I had bigger hopes than they did. New York, Columbia, and, ultimately, Bridge Street provided the types of opportunities I felt God wanted me to have, and life between these three places would refine my talents and skills in ways life in Buffalo couldn't.

I felt at home—more in my proper space—when walking the streets of New York. It was culturally rich, and it felt to me like every opinion and perspective, every major development, everything that was important to human life was in New York—particularly Manhattan. Things I'd heard about and read about were imprinted on the city. It was a micro-version of the United States, containing within a small geographical area the sociocultural, political, economic, and religious makeup of a nation. New York City wasn't only that; it was also a microcosm of the world—capturing the imagination of a global population and serving as a point of entry for those wanting more than merely to imagine the United States.

The city had a rich history that played out in the life of African Americans. Major churches and religious movements called New York home, and cultural developments that transformed the world—music, literature, architecture— lived in places like Harlem.

Manhattan had its pockets of economic struggle and political neglect where city infrastructure showed its years and the wear and tear associated with so many cold winters and hot summers faded paint and compromised exteriors. Even if one were underground, on the subway or on a bus, it was fairly easy to mark out the shifts in wealth and influence—where the "haves" got off the bus or train marked a boundary. On the East Side they didn't move beyond 96th Street, and on the West Side they got off the train at the edge of Harlem. In contrast, Times Square was a synergy of light and activity, a central spot where people converged before moving on to something else—a show, a restaurant, a gallery, some shopping. However, when I arrived as a student, Times Square was also the red-light district, near the bus station, where pimps preyed on the vulnerable and where whiffs of desperation lingered in the streets just outside the peep shows and adult entertainment establishments.

Despite the seedy elements and countless stories of demise and degradation, Manhattan had a reputation for cultural outlets, fine dining, and Broadway, and wealth centered around areas like Central Park West, Park Avenue, and Madison Avenue, where the moneymakers lived and shopped. It was that dimension of Manhattan that caught attention and, for many, marked it as the borough worthy of admiration and envy.

Even though I understood Manhattan represented sin in profound and blatant ways, I still enjoyed it and wanted to be there. I could evangelize lost souls but also take in the city's wonders. I recognize the paradox in this—save sinners while appreciating the secular dimensions of life.

Bedford-Stuyvesant was a study in contrasts. There were good people in that section of Brooklyn, and I felt comfortable there. People worked hard, but poverty overshadowed that portion of New York's geography. It wasn't Brooklyn Heights, where the television family headed by Bill Cosby lived in a million-dollar home. It wasn't an area of the city dominated by specialty shops and the like, the way Park Slope now looks. No, I was there during the birth of crack cocaine; the signs of it being sold and used were hard to miss. Once beautiful limestone and brownstone buildings were boarded up and of no use to anyone other than the occasional homeless person or crackhead. Gangs carved up the region for drug sales, and people tried to keep their families safe in places where violence could easily and quickly break out.

Still, Bedford-Stuyvesant had a rough beauty. There was a diversity of people of African descent, and the food, clothing, languages, and other signs of their heritage were evident and celebrated in a raucous way—from parades to more culturally particularized and smaller events. There was more racial and cultural energy in that small section of the city than I'd encountered in the entire city of Buffalo.

There were big differences between Manhattan and Bedford-Stuyvesant, and I spent some of my free time trying to get a handle on what both offered.

*   *   *

I didn't have much money, so I spent a lot of time moving around on foot: looking up at the buildings (as discreetly as possible, so as not to look like a tourist who could be robbed easily), looking into shop windows, sitting on benches, and people watching. New York City was rough and dirty, but it had a refinement and temperament that I found completely and utterly compelling. It was much louder than I was used to, coming from Buffalo, and the pace was faster, but I enjoyed it. People worried about crime, but being alert and exercising common sense were enough. Having on the "full armor of God," as one of God's ministers, was an added layer of protection.

Being in New York pushed me to see the world differently. While walking the city I felt this confrontation with my homegrown ideas, and I was challenged intellectually in school to rethink my assumptions and my status. I wasn't special or exceptional on that score; everyone had been set apart and perceived as being unique prior to arriving on the Upper West Side of Manhattan. I had the added challenge of coming from a school were academics were advanced but held suspect, and where the regulations of the church shadowed the classroom.

I couldn't assume my professors believed what I believed and that the Christian faith wasn't understood as the ultimate test of truth. Heaven and hell were of no concern, and the securing of salvation—unlike in church and at West Seneca Christian—wasn't the ultimate indication of progress and growth. But, like my high school, race factored in.

The first few months of my first year were marked by the same aggressive questions over and over again: "What are your SAT scores?" "Where did you go to high school and were you in AP classes?" "What was your GPA?" All of these questions led to the ones expressed in posture and facial expressions but said out loud only by the most aggressive: "How did *you* get into Columbia? It must have been affirmative action, right?"

I hated these questions; they made me angry and caused doubt. How *had* I gotten in? Was I really up to it? I'd ask myself these questions, although I'd never let anxiety show on my face.

It was tough financially, although, in my last sermon at Agape, I told the people that God would make a way and God would provide. I received aid from the school and the state, but not as much as I might have if my father had cooperated. Although my parents were divorced, my father was required to submit financial information. He refused; he couldn't understand why that school needed to "know his goddamn business." In that resistance I always assumed there was something passive-aggressive. He couldn't tell me what to do, where to go to school, so he'd find another way to make known his belief that I should go to school at home where the costs could be covered. For him, education was education, and a desire to leave Buffalo made no sense. Why do that, just to go to another school that's going to cost more than my home—348 Florida Street—cost? This may have been his reasoning, but from my perspective as a student trying to get my bills covered, he was just being an ass . . . again.

His stubbornness meant that my mother struggled to pay what financial aid didn't cover. Tax refunds each year usually did the trick, but until that money arrived, trying not to overspend was the trick. Shopping was our coping mechanism—a way of dealing with stress. We didn't eat comfort food to cope; instead we bought stuff—a new jacket, shoes, and modest luxury items. My mother showed her concern for me and her effort to be a good parent by getting me things. I'd say "Thank you" because I had been taught to be polite. But I didn't worry about bills. I assumed that, between my mother's paycheck and the little bit of money my father paid in child support (not enough to even feed me, really), things would get covered. If nothing else, we could always fall back on the "God will make a way" mantra-prayer-and-in-severe-cases-fasting strategy of financial management.

Our logic involved an assumption that God wanted God's children to have the best. We were wonderfully made, and God wanted us to have nice things as a way to bring glory and honor to the name of the Lord. We updated this perspective, but it was as old as the spirituals in which religious righteousness and material gain were connected. "All God's Children" or songs referencing the streets of gold in heaven spoke to the ability of my ancestors to see the relationship between salvation and material comfort. Scriptural passages to support this could easily be picked out and thrown about with a firm voice and followed by a "Thank you, Jesus!"

I got pretty good at holding off the bursar's office until my mother's tax refund arrived and we could pay the tuition bill. This tactic, along with the generosity of Bridge Street Church kept my head above my bills. Over my four years at Columbia, my financial survival revolved around ministerial work-for-hire and checks coming from my work-study job at the church.

Juanita Berry was a joy in the church office. I worked for her on different community-related projects, and on Saturdays I'd help her put together hundreds of church bulletins used the next day for service. She could be tough and she spoke her mind, but I don't remember her saying a harsh word that wasn't followed by a knowing smile. She looked out for me, making certain I had time for my schoolwork and a few dollars in my pocket. Any time I preached, Ms. Berry was in the back of the church, smiling and nodding. I'd look for her as I mounted the pulpit those early Sunday services when I was allowed to preach. When I saw her I felt comforted.

I didn't join Bridge Street immediately; in fact, at one point Lucas told me it didn't have to be Bridge Street, but I needed to join a church. It took a while, but eventually I resigned my Agape membership and joined Bridge Street, and immediately people in the church looked out for the young minister. In blessing me they understood God would bless them, but it wasn't that calculated. They were just good people. Friends at church like Jesse Howard and his sister, Melinda Howard, were family, and they helped me make it. I'm not certain why they were so kind and giving; I don't know what they saw in me that warranted their time, attention, and support. They were generous beyond measure. I've never felt as if I've paid them back for this generosity, and this is because I didn't. They looked after me and welcomed me into their world and family without qualification and without reservation.

Jesse and I met during a snowstorm when he came by the parsonage and helped me shovel snow, and from that day on, we were close; it was a quick connection and the friendship built from there. While I was in New York, Jesse and I spent time together. We were good friends—more like brothers. He died much too young.

Fred and Barbara Lucas agreed to let me spend summers in New York living at the parsonage and working at the church. This was ideal for me. I didn't want to go back to Buffalo; I thought doing that would just pull me backward. My friends in Buffalo were important to me, but my future and fulfilling my ambitions (and God's plans for me) were without a doubt more pressing. Nothing would get in the way and, to the extent Buffalo and most things associated with Buffalo—including my girlfriend at the time—were barriers to my advancement, I was more than willing to set them aside. It was a harsh attitude, deeply selfish in a certain way, but I believed it was consistent with what God required of me.

When I wasn't in Bedford-Stuyvesant, hanging out with the black and Latino students from Columbia relieved some of the stress of being a working-class student on what seemed to me a wealthy campus, and of being a cultural outsider on what felt like a Eurocentric campus. Time with them meant familiar conversations, comforting jokes, and comments within a community based on a shared relationship to the larger campus. We were the same in our differences. Students "of color" on campus bonded. Many of us ate together in the cafeteria—a section called the "Lion's Den"—away from the main dining hall. We understood something about each other, shared similar stories and struggles, and enjoyed the company of people who "got it." In addition to this general connection, I made long-standing friends on campus, like Stanley Bernard. We came from similar financial circumstances and felt as if we shared a common goal of surviving the worst aspects of life on the Columbia campus.

That thin envelope containing the letter inviting me to leave my familiar world and become part of the rarified air of the Columbia campus changed more about my life than I anticipated. There is little I would change about those four years at Columbia. Intellectually it was a good place for me, and I've benefited from what "Columbia blue" offered and have many fond thoughts of my alma mater.

There was much about Columbia that assumed privilege and resources we didn't have. Even the way the geography of the city was presented isolated us from what was familiar. During orientation and then through more casual conversations on campus, I got the impression that Columbia was worlds from Harlem. It was the Upper West Side (not Harlem), and the connotations related to this understanding were huge. I was warned that Harlem was a dangerous place and that it should be approached with caution and care. It was difficult being told to be leery of people who looked like me *because* they looked like me.

I started my four years at Columbia deeply religious and assumed I would be a religion major. I was a preacher-in-training; why not learn more about Christianity and other traditions? Learning more about other traditions would give me the skills necessary to dissect them and prove the superiority of my faith. I also planned to spend time at Union Theological Seminary, located across the street from Columbia. Ministers received training there, so I thought it made sense to hang around there as much as I could in order to get a sense of what theological education was all about. Some of the students there showed me kindness and let me hang out with them, encouraging me in my studies and introducing me to their faculty.

During the AME annual conference that year, held at Bridge Street, one of these students introduced me to theologian James Cone, considered the "father" of black theology of liberation and also a member of the denomination. Cone was a centerpiece of the Union Theological Seminary faculty. It was a famous place, having been the intellectual home to some of the greatest theological minds of the twentieth century—Reinhold Niebuhr, Paul Tillich, Dietrich Bonhoeffer, and now Cone. I was beginning to read his writings, and I found them inspiring. They spoke to me, and I found myself highlighting virtually every word on every page, with side comments in the margins that represented my effort to affirm his words and speak back to him.

I told him that I loved religion and wanted to study it, that I couldn't get enough of it. I expected Cone to affirm my plan. Instead, his response was straightforward and sobering: "You are developing a false sense of spirituality that isn't practical in the real world. . . . You should study sociology or anthropology."

That statement felt like a punch in the stomach, but it made me think. Was I focusing on the wrong markers of my calling and of my faith? Was there still something about my approach to education that was too West Seneca Christian in nature? Had I been assuming that there was no distinction worth making between spiritual yearning and my academic trajectory?

Cone wasn't trying to push me away from my sacred duty, and he wasn't working outside the safety of the church community. In response to his advice, I decided to major in sociology and minor in religion. Courses in urban sociology really captured my imagination. Projects for those courses took me out of the classroom and gave me a way to take Harlem seriously. I also thought these courses would give me a way of thinking about the city, its sociocultural geography, and would help me to formulate questions and perspectives on life that could inform my ministry. I reasoned sociology would give me a way of describing the world I wanted to transform for Christ. Of course, it wouldn't be this easy or this straightforward. I couldn't move from biblical passages to city passageways.

My high school teachers always made it clear they were *Christian* school-teachers. That label—Christian—wasn't mentioned by any of my instructors at Columbia, and it was clear to me that claiming it myself wouldn't result in any type of perceivable advantage. In fact, it was more likely to be met with pity or a "Who cares?" This is not to say I was alone in my faith but that religion was a personal decision with no implications for the Columbia college classroom. The Bible didn't matter in the same way on campus; even in biblical studies courses it was simply literature, the stories and fantasy of a group with limited historical reach. And so I had to relearn how to learn. This had implications for both my academic life and my ministry.

I wanted to be like Fred Lucas, a respected minister entrenched in the community and addressing neighborhood concerns. Bridge Street gave me the opportunity to work on my own version of ministry. I participated in the order of service—giving one of the scripture readings, leading congregational prayer, welcoming visitors, or inviting the congregation to the altar for individual prayer. One member of the staff might preach the early service or one of the weekday services. Unlike at Agape, I also had responsibility for visiting the sick and shut-ins. I served them Communion, listened to them reflect on the church, and prayed with them—all in the presence of one of the church stewards assigned to accompany me. I also served as a youth minister, working with junior high and high school students in an afterschool program and managing a basketball program.

The member of the church who owned and operated a funeral home would invite me to conduct funerals. I'd sometimes give a short eulogy, ride with him to the cemetery, do the committal of the body ("Ashes to ashes, dust to dust . . ."), and ride back home with a few dollars in payment in my pocket. I also did some of the Saturday weddings that Reverend Lucas couldn't manage, along with the occasional wedding during the week. That money paid some of my bills and bought a few extra items.

My full-fledged ministerial work came when Reverend Lucas went on vacation, as most ministers did in August, and I was in his office during the week "managing" things. It didn't involve a terrible amount of actual work, but I was the figurehead. When calls came in or requests were made, the church secretary sent them my way.

It wasn't as if I was positioned to make big decisions, but I did sit behind his desk and imagine myself a prominent minister. Being one, however, required work outside the walls of the church. It meant being able to manage deals that brought resources and opportunity into the church and the church's neighborhood. Business savvy was beneficial, and a sense of the politics of the city was vital if the church was going to save souls within the context of a revived community. Lucas exposed me to the political-business side of church work by taking me to meetings with city officials, including the mayor and congressmen, and I'd watch from the sidelines to see how he interacted with them.

I was learning ministry, and at the end of my first year of college I would take a big step in my credentialing for ministry. I'd gone through the Ministerial Institute, passed each required dimension of the program, and had survived the questioning by religious leaders in my district. As a result of this, I was to be ordained.

The day of the ordination, church members from the area, ministers, presiding elders, and the bishop gathered. It was a rite of passage—an opportunity to ritualize our progress and to announce to the larger congregation our new place within the formal ministerial ranks of the church. One of the outstanding preachers gave a sermon as a marker of the style and strength of delivery for which we should strive. The sermon spoke to our new position and the obligations and responsibilities associated with it, warning us to be serious and dedicated in the tasks before us as official ministers of the church.

Service culminated with those of us to be ordained led to the altar. We knelt down, and the ministers we'd selected as our inner circle, our models and mentors, placed a hand on us to bless us as the bishop brought us into the connection, into the itinerate ministry. The ministers laying hands on us were to represent the type of ministry we hoped to have, the type of connection to God we desired. But there was something political about it as well: could I afford to offend by excluding as a member of the inner circle a minister from whom I might need a favor or endorsement? No.

Becoming a deacon was a major step in my training. In theory I could be assigned to pastor a church, although this wasn't very likely. More important, I was now officially called "Reverend." Prior to ordination I was simply "Minister." "Reverend" had a different weight to it and came with obligations more deeply rooted in allegiance to the denomination, its creeds and doctrines. Once people were ordained and called Reverend, there was a different sense of spiritual stature, one that played into the sense of masculinity I'd learned to follow earlier in my calling.

Women were ordained, but ours was a church still slow to recognize the right of women to be involved in ordained ministry. And with women representing the vast majority of the denomination's membership, this had both real and symbolic importance. While ordination meant that I was at least theoretically positioned for a major pulpit after "paying my dues," it was unlikely that a woman with the same skill set would be encouraged to think the same thing, to assume the same possibility.

Women tended to serve in subordinate roles within large churches, or they might pastor small or moderately populated churches. There was some critique of this problem within the church, and some of those making this challenge most energetically were friends and acquaintances of the Lucases. Some were still in school at that point, but they would become major players in both the church and the academy. Yet the church was rooted in a tradition that ran contrary to this type of gender inclusiveness. Instead, it abided by the difference of gender as real, God-ordained, and with consequences that benefited men and confined women to those functions of the family and church more domestic in nature; that is, as caregivers for both families at home and families in the church. I was now a *man* of God, accountable for always behaving in that way, and teenage slips were judged. I was supposed to have answers to all the pressing questions; I was to have solutions for those people, including adults, who came to the church for counseling. I was to have an unusually high—certainly higher than parishioners—ability to focus on God's will and an increased sensitivity to God's voice.

Young reverends were also highly desired life partners. Many invitations to dinner involved meeting daughters and granddaughters because of a common belief that a preacher makes a good husband. Navigating those landmines was difficult. I didn't want to hurt the feelings of the various matchmakers, but if I wasn't interested . . . I wasn't interested. And, even if the young woman did spark my interest, as a minister, there were few and always highly prescribed ways my interest could be expressed. Jesus first!

I was ordained and accountable to the church, with all its flaws and short-comings. I was a son of the church and had agreed to submit to the authority of God first and the bishop second as the administrative head of my partic-ular district (the First Episcopal District, the oldest district). As a deacon, I could marry people, bury people, and baptize people. I couldn't consecrate the Communion elements, but I could distribute Communion once Reverend Lucas or one of the other elders (the second level of ordination) consecrated them.

Communion on the first Sunday of each month was a time-consuming process, during which all who considered themselves worthy—sins forgiven and no malice—participated in the sacrifice of Christ through the commem-oration of his body and blood. Unlike Roman Catholics, we didn't believe in transubstantiation; we didn't think the Communion bread and wine became the actual body and blood of Christ. They were symbolic, and my job was to distribute either the wine or the bread. It alternated. "This is the body of Christ shed for you and for many . . ." Or "This is the blood of Christ shed for the remission of sins . . ."

I'd say my lines and hand the kneeling person, who held their right palm up on top of the left palm, either a small glass of wine or a wafer. This process could take an hour to make certain everyone present and interested received Communion.

Becoming an AME church itinerate minister didn't involve great, formal theological insights. It wasn't as if I woke up the day after my ordination and had increased clarity concerning the meaning of the Bible and the theological ideas embedded in it and in church doctrine. I knew no more as an ordained minister than I'd known as simply a minister licensed to preach.

What I believed about God, about sin, about the world, about Christ, about the Holy Spirit, about moral evil, and so on hadn't radically changed. Those things hadn't really been tested. As part of the ordination process, I'd been quizzed on my knowledge of church history and doctrine, but fine points of theological argument were assumed to be in place. Beyond that, many of the church leaders didn't know any more than I did. It wasn't as if they all had formal theological training or an interest in complex theological ideas. When pressed on hot theological topics, it wasn't unusual for ministers to say, "My people aren't ready." With time, I took this as code for "I don't know anything about this" or "Addressing this could cost me members and money, so I'll leave it alone."

Ministry involves a sad, and rarely discussed, reality: If you were a good preacher and had charisma, having theological and religious depth weren't necessary. They might be a nice addition, but one could be very successful in the church without them. And, when pushed on any issue, a good offense was the best defense: Put responsibility for the issue on the person raising the question; make having that question an issue of limited faith or an illegitimate challenge to authority. Ostracize and isolate the unruly and, what's more, get them to embrace this marginalization as a consequence of some sort of wrongdoing on their part.

These were all tricks of the trade—lessons learned by conversation and observation. But keeping these tools effective and relevant meant keeping this information away from church laity. The membership had to believe there was something special about the preacher that sanctioned the preacher's work. Without this buy-in, the delicate hierarchy of the church could be severely damaged, and there was too much at stake to allow this to happen.

Balancing my youth and the assumed wisdom of a minister was tricky but necessary to maintain the confidence and commitment of the membership.

This wasn't the only difficult tension to negotiate. When not in church, but in class or in conversation with students, the distinction between the academy and the church became clear to me in a way West Seneca Christian had blurred intentionally. The easy dichotomies I'd been taught at that school and the clear distinction between the saved and the unsaved reinforced at my church weren't easy to maintain after all. The reality was more complex than either West Seneca Christian, Agape, or Bridge Street wanted me to believe.

Chapter Eight

WAIT FOR THE NEXT TRAIN

I was expected to use my spiritual power to get Columbia students to Bridge Street. Once they were there, Fred Lucas would do the rest. It didn't quite work out that way, and, truth be told, I didn't put much effort into evangelizing on campus. Doing that felt uncomfortable in a way it hadn't in Buffalo.

Most of the students I met weren't willing to get up early on Sunday, after a rough Saturday night, to journey to Brooklyn for a church service. If they were interested in church, there were plenty within walking distance—no need for two trains and then a walk.

Sunday mornings were hard; I felt this every time I got up early and made my way to Brooklyn. So many Sundays I wanted to just sleep, maybe do a little work, and relax. Worship took up much of the day with an early service, the main service, and sometimes an afternoon service as well. The food between them was great, and I ate my share—sitting up on the platform in the fellowship hall reserved for ministers. But church was still an all-day affair that gave Mondays a rough start.

Although this Sunday ritual was long and difficult, more pressing was the dissonance between my faith and my education I was beginning to feel, whether in the pulpit or on campus. In my religious studies classes, I encountered religious traditions, including my own, in a way that humanized them by pointing out the historical as opposed to trans-historical origins and concerns guiding them. I was confronted with definitions of religion that were earthly and that pulled at the spiritual assumptions with which I'd arrived on campus and that fueled my work at Bridge Street.

The mysteries of the faith were fading for me.

Some of this information I could deal with by assuming there were things the human mind couldn't fathom: God's wisdom is foolishness to humans.

However, it was difficult to condemn to hell my campus friends, people who didn't believe in God or who didn't see the need for the church and its salvation. Some of them placed higher ethical and moral demands on themselves than did some of the church people I encountered. Even if my secular friends weren't saved, they were still my friends. This ran contrary to what I'd been taught about distancing myself from evil to avoid sin. But according to what I'd been taught in high school and in the church, these people were unsaved and would be punished by God. How could God punish them *and* reward those who were abusive and devious but who were in the church?

Everything seemed to involve some type of pecking order "ordained" by God but without any clear rationale. God loved David, but David broke the rules. Jesus gave Peter control over the keys to the kingdom, but Peter denied him and ran off to protect himself from potential harm. He wanted to be like Jesus . . . but not too much like Jesus. Mary Magdalene remained steadfast, took care of the body of Christ, was first to proclaim Jesus rose from the dead—and the church labeled her a whore. None of this made sense, but that didn't matter because we couldn't know the mind of God; we had to follow, based not on logic but on faith. And this was more important for the ministers of Christ than any others in my church world. It was unacceptable for ministers to have doubts that weren't followed up quickly with strong faith and biblical answers.

Trying to hold together my sense of salvation and my regard for my secular friends was a challenge, particularly because of the questions they asked about my belief: How do you know there was a virgin birth? That makes no medical sense, and why would it be necessary for your faith anyway? Why would God allow original sin, demand payment, and then pay the price through the death of a part of God? If only God was free of taint and capable of satisfying God's need for restitution, why even bring people into the equation? Isn't it ridiculous to think the earth can be explained by any means other than evolution? And what do you make of the contradictions and inconsistencies in the Bible? Doesn't what we know about the Bible indicate it is just another piece of human literature drawn from human imagination?

What I once perceived as clear and eternal boundaries were being exposed as porous. Was I losing Jesus, or was I simply becoming aware of the earthly nature of my religious commitments? The questions confronting me made me a bit shaky spiritually, but they weren't enough for me to leave the faith. My sense of right and wrong was being damaged. I fought feelings of uncertainty, assuming this was a spiritual test. If I passed through these trials, I would have a strong and powerful ministry.

Still, I couldn't condemn to hell people who seemed kind and just, and so my theology began to change in order to address this dilemma.

Perhaps it was best to understand God as having the ability to move through a variety of channels to bring people to salvation? Perhaps other traditions contained an element of truth that could bring sinners to repentance? Or maybe there were fine points to God's intent that we simply couldn't capture by means of human logic? Perhaps it was important to simply be good to people, to treat others properly, and God would do what God pleased in light of this kindness? There was so much wrong in the world, and I was getting a good dose of that in my sociology classes, so any good act had to please God in some way, shape, or form. Right?

On campus, I was pushed and grilled, and I didn't have good responses. What I said to these challenges didn't go over like similar claims did in church. My critics seemed unshaken by my commitment to the Christian faith. I wanted to cling to faith as the final answer to all human questions, but that didn't stop the questioning coming my way.

I felt myself losing my grip on the certainty of my religion. I had the Holy Spirit, but there weren't the same signs of it in my work at Bridge Street that there had been at Agape. I didn't speak in tongues and have prophecy stem from it; I didn't dance in the spirit like I had at Agape. I was less emotional in my worship. There was less visible excitement coming from me about ministry.

I wanted to blame Bridge Street, to charge it with being less spirit-filled than Agape—that its old gospel choir songs and stately processions were cutting the spirit out of worship, and as a result, I was experiencing the effects of this situation. That defense was just smoke and mirrors because the issue was with me. The hard questions and the resulting shifts in my theology were taking a toll on my faith.

I had to live two lives—one marked by deep questioning and uncertainty and the other requiring that I at least come across as being steadfast and unshakable. I needed to seem confident in order to avoid shaking the faith of the more fragile members of the congregation.

This was a heavy burden, and I felt it keenly. But then again, I assumed God did not put more on us than we can bear. This was a kind of religious version of "that which does not kill us makes us strong." Without tribulation, righteousness and proper spiritual health cannot be achieved. Or there was always the possibility that Satan was trying to weaken my faith. But . . . this could all be a trial God placed on me as punishment for wrongdoing.

Suffering was inevitable. If even God had to endure suffering through Jesus the Christ, there was little reason to think humans could escape it. The question was how to understand, manage, and incorporate suffering into our religious worldview, to make religious sense of it. Stakes were high; souls were at risk, and I was struggling to be at ease with my responsibilities outside and inside the church.

At Bridge Street I worked with some young people for whom life was fragile and the possibility of a short life was all too real. I performed funeral services—not a lot but enough—for some of the young people in New York who died as a result of gang violence and the drug trade. These services were typically held at funeral homes rather than churches, and I was instructed to "get them in and out," not to prolong the service beyond thirty minutes or so, and not to get the mourners too excited. No need to increase the chances of additional violence around the funeral home due to grief (and thoughts of revenge) fueled by my remarks.

I remember the faces of those young people in caskets, and I remember the looks on the faces of those gathered to mourn them. Those in the folding chairs didn't look surprised; they didn't express confusion. This all seemed a normal and accepted component of their world. My job for thirty minutes was to bring their world and my religious world together, all for a few dollars in compensation.

I didn't share much with these other young people. We didn't have a lot in common, but we did share an appreciation for hip-hop, particularly rap music. My experiences weren't the same as those described in the lyrics, but hip-hop spoke to me. It became a filter through which I ciphered much of my campus experience. It offered a language, new ways of communicating the underbelly of urban life, the patterns of living that kept ministers busy. I loved the aesthetic of hip-hop and craved rap music. But there were ways that hip-hop culture reinforced the tensions and paradoxes already growing between my religious life and my academic life. Hip-hop marked out my class privilege and what that meant for how I thought, what I assumed as the stuff of life, and my relationship to mainstream American life. I was privileged by my connection to Columbia and by my position within the church. Listening to Grandmaster Flash and the Furious Five and other artists, my identity was more fractured than I was comfortable to admit.

I had no problem with it being worldly music, nor did the raw language and imagery bother me. It was my connection to the social privilege it challenged and the role my religion played in much of its angst that gave me pause. Hip-hop was more like the blues that signified religious beliefs than the spirituals that informed the content of my faith. I thought my religion provided liberation, provided an answer to life's worries, but hip-hop raised questions about this assumption.

Adults in my church didn't necessarily take their lead from hip-hop culture, but they had their own set of issues and concerns. The adults, not all but enough of them, struggled to keep it together, to find meaning in life and to provide for themselves and those they loved. Others were financially secure, yet they wrestled with emotional and psychological challenges. Some might have felt guilty about their success in light of how others struggled. They didn't live in the depths of this troubled neighborhood but commuted from more stable locations, and they remembered this as they fought for parking spots near the church. God promised them a good life in exchange for obedience and their tithe, but receiving this blessing wasn't without buyer's remorse. What about those who did what the prosperous in the congregation did, but without the same rewards and opportunities? Was there something lacking in their living of the faith?

The order of service, the songs, the prayers, greeting people with a "holy kiss" on the cheek, the sermons, Communion, all seemed limited in their reach. I wasn't certain church accomplished much more than a temporary emotional lift without a substantial difference in daily life. What my religion understood as faith required a happy face in front of tragedy, a commitment to joy despite the circumstances. Faith is the answer before the question is asked.

People seemed fine for as long as they were in church, but each week held similar struggles, and they came back to church each Sunday to wrestle with the same disappointments and concerns week after week. Maybe what we ministers provided were spiritual bandages that had to be reapplied each Sunday? My typical responses seemed to miss the point. At best, I answered questions people weren't asking and avoided the pertinent questions by turning them over to God with a concerned look on my face and perhaps a hand on the shoulder or an offer to pray with and for them.

Could a minister say, "I don't know" as more than a sermonic device ultimately resulting in a "But God knows, and God has told me . . ."?

My education was multilayered, taking place on the campus through casual observation and through my church work. It was an ongoing process during the day, and my dreams were often an extension of that process, a type of resting rehearsal of problems and potential solutions with some of the restrictions of my conscious life eliminated.

I didn't know how to fully articulate this struggle, so my response often was simply to miss enough of church service on Sunday to avoid having to be in the pulpit. With suit on and Bible in tow, I'd cross the campus to the subway station at West 116th and Broadway. Moving down the stairs I'd think about church and what I was expected to do and say; I'd rehearse the small talk between services and prepare myself to pretend I was happy to be there and to be fully equipped with spiritual energy. I'd take my position on the subway platform. I'd wait for the train to arrive . . . and let it pass and wait for the next train. I'd get on the third train, and I'd make my way to the stop where I'd transfer to the "A" Train headed to Brooklyn. The process at that station was the same—let trains go by until I was certain I couldn't get to church in time to help with the service. Once I arrived at my stop in Brooklyn, I'd leave the station and walk slowly to the church.

Service was already under way by the time I arrived.

Reverend Lucas might be annoyed I was late, but he couldn't ask me to say a prayer, or read a scripture, or participate in any way.

After service I'd go up front and apologize: "I'm sorry, Reverend Lucas . . . it was the train."

Yes, it was the train, but I didn't include the fact that I'd missed trains intentionally so I wouldn't have to go behind the altar where the ministers positioned themselves.

I didn't lie, but I didn't say everything I could have said. I let him, and anyone else close enough to hear, believe that there had been a problem with the train schedule—maybe a delay because of a problem with the tracks. The subway was in need of maintenance, and so my story didn't come across as being too hard to believe. And no one would check into it.

I was free from obligations for that day, so I'd sit passively and watch the service. Schoolwork often kept me free of afternoon services, and I'd make my way back to Manhattan. On other occasions, when there wasn't an afternoon service to attend, I'd spend the rest of the day with my church friends hoping they wouldn't treat me like a minister but as just one of the guys—maybe we'd catch a movie, or get a meal at a diner, or just walk around. I enjoyed those times because I could just be Tony, without the robe or the title.

Sometimes, not to raise suspicion, I'd call Lucas and tell him that school-work meant I couldn't make it to service. He couldn't object to me getting an education. It still seemed as if I was involved and fulfilling my ministerial responsibilities, and this is because I kept pace with my non-Sunday service activities with youth ministry. I continued to smile when I saw people from the church, and I greeted them with as much joy and confidence as I could manage.

Salvation was still real for me. We needed to get right with God, but that personal dimension was no longer sufficient. Sunday service was about bringing together groups of people who were really only concerned with individual development. We simply worked through this individualism in the company of others. The sermon might mention community responsibilities, but after the sermon was the "call to Christian discipleship," where the truth and power of the sermon was measured against the number of people who came forward to join the church. After all the group singing, the greetings, the inclusive prayers, and the sermon, the bottom line was personal transformation.

How did my Christianity function in the world? Was it really *the* way? These questions didn't mean I was an agnostic or humanist—and they certainly didn't mean I was an atheist. A more accurate description was that I was moving—reluctantly and with great worry—from an evangelical theology and religion to a more liberal theology and faith. I still believed in God, but I was growing to believe God wouldn't break into human history and *make* anything happen. Rather, God inspired and used humans to bring about God's will. It was a version of my mother's "God has no hands but your hands, no legs but your legs" sense of God. The divine is present in and bound up with the human—from the very beginning, when God gave the first humans a piece of God's self as the spark of life; through the blending in blood and pain of God and humanity in the birth of Jesus the Christ; and continuing by means of salvation and the indwelling of the Holy Spirit. The sacred is embedded in the secular.

Thinking this way, as a college student, I wasn't surrendering a belief that God is distinct from humans; rather I was beginning to recognize that the divine was only knowable within the context of material life, in the stuff of our daily lives. I continued to believe that God is good, powerful, and just. The basic outline of God provided in scripture was true to me and was verified—I hoped with all my faith—in the realities of human life.

No burning bushes or booming voices from on high, no trembling rooms or spirits in the form of doves. No radical breaks in our ordinary world that couldn't be explained as anything other than a miracle. Human handprints and footprints in history were clear. What humans did to destroy and also enhance life was easily knowable. God's handprint or footprint on our world wasn't as evident as I once believed, and the efforts of preachers like me to point out these prints for the sake of no real tangible gains was losing its appeal.

The Bible was the major tracking device for finding God. It was a filter used to distill our experiences so as to find in them the presence of God. Otherwise we were alone in the world and left to our own skills. I believed this, but I began to think differently concerning how and where to find God: I was moving from a preoccupation with personal salvation as the task of the church and as the preacher's primary focus, to social transformation—a real response to people's pressing needs as the litmus test for the faith.

My faith wasn't on life support, at least it wasn't consistently at that critical stage. The situation wasn't so extreme, although at moments it felt that way. I had my times of strong questioning, but they were followed by glimpses of relief and certainty. I was still a Christian but one who had finally encountered the world without my protective blinders on. I was taking them off and seeing people, holding to the Christian faith, and needing to transform both people and my faith for the better.

As much as I disliked it, I was feeling an increasingly urgent need to question everything, to pull my faith apart in order to put it back together with a profound and new strength and significance.

My sense of the importance of people within religion, theology, and the church was growing and taking up some of the room that had once been occupied only by the all-powerful, all-knowing, and history-wrecking God.

I was still suspicious toward people. My family dynamics, along with what could be a nasty side on the part of church people, affirmed the need for this, but I was also becoming increasingly dependent on people to explain God and God's movement in the world. People mattered, not just because they occupied the pews, but more importantly because they, and other life-forms, were all we could know through our senses. To the extent I said anything about God, told stories about God's work laid out in scripture, it was funneled through people and places—through flesh and blood.

My evangelical thinking had meant privileging the spirit and the spiritual in a way that found flesh and blood a problem to solve through prayer, fasting, and disciplined attention to scripture. This was all changing for me, and I was developing a secularism intertwined with my religious commitments. It was an awkward and unstable development—but going back to a pure evangelical, forget-the-world stance wasn't possible.

I maintained my commitment to trans-historical truths and the idea that religion involved a unique type of experience with cosmic forces, but I was connecting this belief to concern with the ordinary dimensions of life. I was confronting the secular as more than something to fear; for me it meant a way to see, to actually see and appreciate, human life.

I maintained my interest in a career within the church, but what that meant was shifting and changing. College was coming to a close, and I had to prepare for the next phase. I spent late evenings taking the GRE preparation course paid for by the financial aid office at the university. There was less time for me to get together with church friends because I needed to prepare applications. Some of them understood, but a few didn't. Their frustration with my plan wasn't a concern for me because I had to look beyond them and keep my focus on my life and career. Nothing and no one would hamper me.

Like the "social gospel" I was beginning to read, I would meld spiritual renewal with betterment of material existence. I'd need to read more, to learn more about how others shaped and worked out their callings. I hoped something about their stories would provide me with tools for growing my own ministry and my own theology sufficient for the needs of the people I'd encounter in my future pastorates. That was my plan: to receive theological training and prepare myself to preach liberation in a way that was transformational.

My grades wouldn't be a problem, but I'd need help with the personal statement to be included in my application. My oldest sister had helped with college, but I didn't turn to her for help with these applications. Fred and Barbara Lucas read over numerous drafts and helped me refine it. Fred, although he graduated from Harvard, put no pressure on me to apply there. He just wanted me to get a theological education. As one of his "sons in the ministry," the proper training along with the benefits of his reputation could mean a substantial role for me in the hierarchy of the church someday. Virtually any divinity school or seminary could be a proper step in that direction.

I submitted my applications to Harvard, Princeton, Union, and a few others. There was enough to keep me busy, so I didn't get nervous about applications until shortly before I knew letters of acceptance and rejection would be sent out.

Applying to schools forced me to think about places I'd feel comfortable living.

I had little experience with the West Coast, having visited my brother and sister Linda there, but I didn't find that area of the country compelling. Having to worry about which colors to wear, or my brother having to arrange for one of the local kids to "keep me safe" in gang-infested areas of Los Angeles was too much for me. I didn't know the South beyond a couple of childhood trips back to Halifax, North Carolina, the home of my grandparents. Nothing about those trips struck me as a good reason to want to live in the South. Even rough winters seemed part of life and no big deal—certainly no reason to leave the Northeast, where there were plenty of opportunities for a young, ambitious, and capable preacher.

As I waited to hear from the universities and completed my classes, I talked with some of the students at Union Theological Seminary. I wasn't as far along as most of them. I was younger and didn't belong to the same network. But I gathered from my meetings and meals with them as much as I could. I took seriously the readings they suggested. And I still use some of the language I learned from them—particularly when it comes to encouraging people to read by saying, "You'll want to put that book on your summer reading list. You'll thank me in the fall."

These other students also gave me a way of thinking about theological education—the amount as well as the type of work required, the kinds of conversations that took place and the ways information from the classroom and the library could be interjected into ministry. I needed those skills, but I didn't want to stop there. I'd also decided for certain that my training would extend beyond the professional degree for ministry and would include a PhD. Part of my interest in the PhD was pure greed—if the PhD was the highest mark of intellectual attainment, I wanted it. But there was also something deeper and more meaningful to my goal: with that degree I would teach at a college or university part time and pastor an AME church full time. One foot in the academy and one in the church.

Most of the ministers I met didn't have a PhD, although some had secured a Doctor of Ministry degree. Others simply purchased a robe with the three velvet bars on each sleeve indicating the doctorate, and let people assume they had earned what the robe represented. The people in that latter group simply wanted to have a double handle: Rev. Dr. in front of the name, like Rev. Dr. Martin L. King Jr. They wanted the "pastor is a servant of God *and* smart" statement that goes along with being "Rev. Dr." It gave them status, whether earned or not, which spoke to both spiritual prowess and high-level educational achievement. I found that practice disrespectful, and to the extent it continues to take place within church circles, it is a mark of their failure to take advantage of what reason and logic might offer. I believe they, on some level, fear what the deep questioning associated with higher education might do to their assumptions and comfort.

I was determined to be different.

I needed to get out of New York and away from my church family in Brooklyn to have the emotional distance necessary for thinking through my theological and ministerial problems. As my grandmother would say, I was "between a rock and a hard place."

Chapter Nine

THEY DON'T REALLY TRAIN PREACHERS

The letters of acceptance started coming in, and after weighing my options, I decided to attend Harvard Divinity School.

When Reverend Lucas found out I was serious about attending Harvard, he and one of the church trustees drove me to the campus to take a look around and to meet with Preston Williams—the only African American tenured professor at the Divinity School. In his office, shortly after sitting down, Williams announced that I had been accepted into the Divinity School. He congratulated me, and we started to talk. I asked questions about the curriculum, field education placements, and other aspects of the program. Lucas answered some of my questions and asked some of his own. On our way back later that day, before we'd even reached New York, I'd made my decision. I, as Barbara Lucas put it, was going to be a "Harvard man."

I imagine a lot of people assumed I would go to Union Theological Seminary, study with James Cone, and remain an associate minister (but with more responsibilities and visibility) at Bridge Street. But I felt like the questions and concerns I had couldn't be addressed at Union, at least not as they needed to be, and if I didn't get them out I would explode, or maybe implode. Either way, it wouldn't be a good situation. Harvard would be different. The professors had the ability to push me to grow, and black church culture in Boston-Cambridge offered what I thought would be fertile training ground.

During a Sunday morning service Reverend Lucas had me stand as he

137

announced I would be leaving at the end of the summer to start my theological studies at Harvard Divinity School. My Bridge Street family cheered
and clapped, proud at my success and glad they'd played a role in making it
happen. After service, people congratulated me, hoping that things would go
well but sad I would be leaving. Some worried about the challenges to faith a
place like Harvard could pose. This was matched by an assumption that God
would protect God's preacher from harm.

I finished up the school year and graduated. The church planned to rent
buses and be present on campus to cheer me on, but I had to break the bad
news that I had only two tickets and the Columbia campus was closed to those
without tickets. I gave one to my mother and the other to Fred Lucas, who'd
played such a big role in my life. It was my way of saying thank you to him to
make up for the many times I'd tried to say it in the past.

I worked at the church for much of that last summer in New York by con-
ducting funerals, weddings, and helping Ms. Berry around the office. It was
also the last summer I'd have with my church friends.

It was finally time to leave. I packed my suitcase and trunk, and Fred Lucas
and the same church trustee who'd made the trip to visit the school drove me to
Cambridge, Massachusetts. We unloaded my belongings from the car, put them
in my room at Rockefeller Hall, said a prayer, and they headed back to New York.

I was anxious, a bit concerned, and at one point wondered if I should have
been in that car with them—and heading to Union Theological Seminary.
The feeling passed, and I unpacked.

One of my most-asked questions, particularly of African American students,
was "Which church do you attend?" Some named a local church. Others seemed
offended by the question, and still others launched into a critique of the church
and their concern only with the academic study of religion. Falling back into old
thought habits, I wondered why those in that last group were there rather than
studying in a Religious Studies Department somewhere. Never saying this to
them directly, I tried to get a sense of their perspective, and from those who were
further along I tried to get the lay of the land—whom to avoid in the classroom,
which courses were "must takes," and how to connect with Boston-Cambridge.

Boston had a reputation for racial animosity, from the period of busing to
the present. There were sections of the city—like South Boston—that were

notorious for this, and I stayed away from them as best I could, particularly as the sun was going down. I'd heard too many stories of race-based attacks to feel comfortable venturing into those areas. Unlike New York, where the lack of space and the large number of people meant contact with "others," life in Boston-Cambridge seemed more provincial. The area may have been a hotbed of radical and liberal thought with respect to the forming of the nation, but that same spirit wasn't present when I arrived.

It wasn't uncommon for me to walk down one of the streets in Boston-Cambridge and hear someone yell out their window, "Nigger!"

Very early on I felt embattled and out of place, with residents questioning why I was there. This was on top of what I experienced as a visceral reaction to university students. Boston-Cambridge lacked the emotional and geographic ease of movement I experienced in Manhattan. I quickly learned how to recognize and how to address the xenophobia I encountered. Despite all this difficulty, I made it through the first year with good grades and a sense that I'd learn a great deal about myself and my faith during the course of my program.

Starting with the end of my first year, summers provided graphic illustrations of the underbelly of Boston life—the anger in some communities and a sense of despair and hopelessness in others.

I'd heard about various programs that hired local university students during the summer. I put on a suit and headed downtown to Action for Boston Community Development in search of one of those jobs. There were more applicants than positions available, but fortunately for me, the assistant director of a conservation and beautification program housed in the building overheard me talking and took me to meet her boss. After looking me up and down, he asked a few questions and hired me. My job was to lead a group of kids—from low-income city families—to work around the city, planting flowers, cleaning lots, and doing other projects meant to increase the visual appeal of the city and to keep them occupied during Boston's hot summers.

We encountered animosity from neighbors and conflicts on the crews depending on which neighborhoods we moved through. Some of the kids, but far from most of them, were in gangs, and a few of them sold drugs. While they'd often deny involvement in gangs and drugs, their absence from work when we went to certain neighborhoods was a clear indicator that they were in fact up to no good. When they got to know me, they might hint at their involvement or flash a wad of bills and jokingly ask if I needed some money. Some of them got into selling drugs as a temporary means of buying things they or their family needed. The risks were high, but the money was good.

The kids had a "dark" image of life, marked by low expectations for themselves and others. Too many of them had no sense they'd experience a long and productive life, not when suffering and death were so evident. When I was growing up, religion was supposed to provide a way to smooth life's sharp edges.

Some of the kids told me they went to church and were involved in the life of their church. Others went to church as performance, particularly on holidays and for special events; it had little bearing on their vision of life. Still others recognized the churches that littered their neighborhoods as a problem—preachers taking money from the poor and doing little to help those in need.

I was at Harvard, and that fact piqued the interests of some of the kids, but I don't remember any of them being impressed with my call to ministry. I had little to say to them on the subject of theology. If I made it through the workday without a major problem with any of them and if they showed up and did their work, I was content. Yes, content, but not happy.

Something was missing with my approach, but their world made me uncomfortable. Should it? I thought it shouldn't. After all, if the ministry of Jesus revolved around hard places of life, shouldn't I develop a comfort with these same sorts of spaces?

My time with these kids pointed out to me shortcomings in my faith and ministry. Religion seemed rarified and impotent. It was fine within the structured situations manufactured by sermons, Bible studies, and youth programs. Outside these scenarios, what I had to say as a "man of God" had little significance, it seemed. That is, when I even had something to say.

I made contacts through my position with the city improvement project that helped me get a job during the academic year with one of the educational programs sponsored by Action for Boston Community Development (ABCD). As a Master of Divinity student and for a few years as a PhD student, I worked as a type of counselor and assistant teacher dealing with high school students at risk. These students were much more informed about life than I was at the time. I felt out of place. I had education, but life experience . . . not so much.

I worked with them one-on-one, tutoring in history, math, and English. I performed other tasks as directed, including helping a group of young men learn how to socialize and to become reasonable and thoughtful adults. Dealing with these young people was a bit tricky at first. I wasn't much older than them, but I was in a position of authority. We had to work out how they should deal with me over time by trial and error.

My boss was also a Harvard student in the School of Education, and he was kind to me, teaching me the ropes and giving me opportunities to be involved. You would think a minister, someone trying to develop and expand his vocational interests, would make the most of these kinds of opportunities. And I tried, but it was difficult. I felt ill-equipped to wrestle with the challenges these students faced.

My boss, his boss, and others I met had a roughness to their thinking about socioeconomic and political issues. They had a pragmatism and realism that flew in the face of my traditional posture of faith, which held that "the Lord will make a way!" That I was a university student didn't necessarily impress them because theories and intellectual arguments didn't get you very far in moving through city bureaucracy. And that I was studying religion seemed a waste of an education; at least this was the impression I got from some of them.

When I was given an opportunity to run the summer program, being a rookie without city government savvy mattered more to my colleagues than my educational background and ministerial commitments. This fact was established early on. So, I didn't talk much about my religious beliefs and vocation; it didn't make for interesting or productive conversation. This was an important lesson for me: faith and education have to prove themselves valuable; their worth won't be assumed in contexts outside the church and the academy. The secular world needed verification of that which the church was willing to assume. And the insulated and privileged nature of Harvard (and other elite schools) allowed the school to play by its own rules.

While I felt a bit isolated in terms of religious commitments and questions, I couldn't feel alone in terms of racial diversity—not at ABCD. On campus it was a different issue. There weren't many African American students on campus, and there was a general agreement that the few of us at Harvard Divinity School needed to connect and work together to make the place tolerable. We came from different parts of the country, were there for different reasons, and had different relationships to religious institutions—but we shared a sense of being marginal to the culture and social arrangements of the school. Or at least we saw strong signs that this was the case: limited attention to African American–centered materials in the curriculum, only one tenured African American on the faculty, and little assistance from the school in connecting to the African American community beyond the campus. Using the black student organization—called Harambee—as our base of operations, we pushed for greater representation in the curriculum and on the faculty. All this meant a centering of my personal and community history in different ways than in college. At Columbia I might complain about the lack of attention to black literature, but at Harvard I was more proactive in pushing the school to recognize the importance of African American spiritual and intellectual resources. In part, I was able to do this because I had a growing awareness of these materials.

I was pulling together cultural awareness and my religious commitments. Beginning to think differently about what it meant to be a black Christian, I had a new appreciation for the tapestry of religious influences that informed what it meant to be religious within the context of African American communities. I brought this concern to my course work through a series of questions I tried to work into my papers and conversations: What impact did African and African American cultures have on the Christian faith? How African was our take on baptism or on being filled with the Holy Spirit? Was dancing in the spirit or speaking in tongues related to spirit possession within African traditional systems? How should I understand and make sense of the hints of hoodoo and conjure that infiltrated church people's movement through life? For example, my family wasn't the only one in which people were told to handle loose hair and nail clippings with care—that we shouldn't let just anyone get hold of them. The assumption was that they were intimate items with power that could be used against us. People who made their way to church on Sundays and who claimed a personal relationship with the Christian God were making these claims about nail clippings, burning candles to achieve certain ends, and so on. What was to be made of these seeming contradictions or at least blending of traditions?

I'd gone to New York with a sense that Christianity was pure and easily differentiated from other traditions. This assumption was damaged as I walked around Brooklyn and Manhattan seeing so many different ways to be religious. In Boston-Cambridge, this realization impacted my academic questions and concerns.

My Christian faith was porous. I understood religious pluralism within African American communities while living in New York, and I understood that people moved between them. But it was through my work at Harvard that I began to appreciate more fully that what took place wasn't simply people moving between traditions or a superficial overlap of some rituals or religious language. What African American religion involved was a blending, more of a synergy between religious languages and ideas than I'd initially thought possible.

I wondered if this shift in my thinking had implications for what I could mean by and claim regarding church ministry. I was becoming more aware and appreciative of the rich and layered cultural background of African Americans, and that softened my approach to the nature of worship and belief within black churches.

I still thought the Christian faith was dynamic, but what started at Columbia continued at Harvard: I was finding it increasingly difficult to condemn those who didn't hold to my particular faith. Every human being, I reasoned, had connections to a reality that extended beyond them. Religion became a way of formalizing and ritualizing those connections. This was a different foundation for faith, but at this stage it was far from firm. The fact is, I was training for the pulpit, for work within a particular religious community, and I wanted to understand ministry as some sort of special calling, a distinct and somehow privileged path.

Master of Divinity students had to take courses in a variety of curricular areas, and I tried to pick classes based on what they would offer me as a resource for the questions that led me to Harvard. Because ethicist Preston Williams was the only tenured African American at the Divinity School, most people assumed black students took all his courses. However, I didn't take many courses with him, but he was involved in my education in other ways. Without ever asking for credit or recognition, he made certain that I and many other students had the

financial resources we needed and the "space" necessary to do our work, whether
we agreed with him or leaned in the direction of James Cone's more aggressive
and black power–framed theology. Williams provided advice when asked and
invited the black students to his home, where he and his wife shared the history
of their time in Cambridge. Those times in their home humanized Harvard for
us and gave us a greater sense of what his experience on that campus was like.
Sitting around their living room also gave us informal lessons on how to survive
Harvard, particularly during times when it could be a very toxic place—marked
by vicious competition between students, faculty fighting battles through students, and the list goes on. While a bit more conservative than most of us considered ourselves to be, Williams looked out for us in his own way and had a
better sense of the place than we did. I didn't follow his perspective on theology
and ethics, but he did give me a way to see the issue of class unlike any way
I'd understood within my church context or as I'd read about it in theological texts. He raised an intriguing question: How does one conceptualize and
work toward liberation in a context where not all the African Americans are
poor? What is the liberative need of the black middle class, the section of the
African American population overlooked by theologians such as Cone? These
were important questions to ponder in that my sense of the pastorate had been
shaped by middle-class aspirations. In fact, my sense of "the work" was dependent on normative middle-class aspirations and values, whether I was thinking
about personal salvation as the display of proper personality characteristics or as
the barriers to community advancement.

Courses on religion and culture gave me a different way of engaging cultural production as the residue, if not the substance, of religious struggling. I
was encouraged to trace the concerns and possibilities of religiosity in the language of cultural expression through recognition of deep connection between
what humans produce and the matters of life and death that constitute the
religious. I'd read American literature as an undergraduate, but not in a way
that really allowed me to decipher the spiritual yearnings embedded in those
texts. I was too preoccupied with church challenges, a general fatigue (like
most students), and plowing through course requirements to catch my breath
and dive into those books. On some level, just having access to the books was
a small form of validation. My culture mattered.

Theology and history of Christian thought courses introduced me to a much more complex world of religious meaning than I even knew possible. Theology as a way of addressing the demands of the contemporary world, as a language for expressing the meaning of the religious within the context of human culture, was the framework for my classes with Gordon Kaufman, who would become my primary adviser. In his lectures and conversation, he made clear the way in which theology wasn't simply about explaining and affirming the faith for people in church pews, but that it also had implications for how we think and behave outside the formal walls of churches. Nothing about my high school years or my church work acknowledged this approach to theology; instead, these two projected theology as the church's servant. Kaufman's question wasn't "How does this preach?" (meaning, "What do we do with this book-learning stuff within church worship?"), and I had to learn to temper my attitude about that view on theology. I also had to figure out how to speak about my religion in ways that made sense in an academic environment in which spiritual matters seemed to be funneled through the desire for an objective take on what religion is and what it seeks to accomplish.

Conservative students would arrive on campus, often thinking they were going to change the place, as I'd thought I was going to change Columbia. They quickly discovered Harvard Divinity School wasn't interested in changing. So, these students either adjusted to the reality of Harvard, were frustrated and in a constant state of prayer, or left for more welcoming places where the Bible ruled.

Placing the Bible alongside other pieces of literature was unthinkable earlier in my life—particularly as a high school student—but it was the standard practice during my Master of Divinity training. Biblical perspectives were discussed as mythological or symbolic, or as literary formulations. Nothing about biblical theology arguments was understood as being beyond questioning, and the Bible wasn't assumed to be more reliable than science and reason. This changed so much about my perspective on the major figures and events of my faith. It was difficult to maintain claims to a virgin birth in light of what I encountered in my readings and in class lectures. God was discussed in more fluid ways that ranged from being simply a symbol, to a limited being working through humans in the world, to a way to name the creative energy of the universe. Salvation in personal terms wasn't a topic of conversation on the campus, and moral evil was discussed in terms of structural wrongdoing addressed through religiously based activism. None of this revolved around a fallen nature. Humans were prone to misconduct, but there were sociocultural rationales given for this as opposed to an assumption of original sin. Hell and heaven weren't high on the agenda, and this was the case even in my preaching class. We discussed and practiced the mechanics of preaching, but we gave no consideration to truth claims. Sermon critiques revolved only around performance, not the truth of our faith statement.

I'd read some progressive thinkers as an undergraduate, but the depth of my exposure and reading increased at Harvard. Saint Augustine was familiar to me, but I also came to know something about his challenger, Pelagius. Augustine argued that the image of God in humans was warped because of original sin and that without special attention from God, through God's grace, we had no hope of redemption. We were intrinsically flawed. Pelagius, on the other hand, argued that God equipped us with all that was necessary to live well, but that we, in Adam, followed a bad example: we are capable humans using the wrong model. I'd thought like Augustine and was influenced indirectly by much of his theological thinking, but at Harvard I found Pelagius compelling.

The irreverence of liberation theologians, religious thinkers who valued the integrity of life above the laws and traditions of the church, also caught my attention. I tried to work through all this in light of the questions and concerns I carried with me from New York. Doing this put me at spiritual risk. It was possible that modifying my beliefs wouldn't be enough. I was exposed to dimensions of the story of the Christian faith that were new and foreign to me, and I was pushed to place this tradition within the context of competing faith claims—each being relevant to those embracing it.

This, I think, is one of the reasons so many church people found theological education so problematic. It wasn't that they were necessarily anti-intellectual. There were schools funded and supported by black churches. Instead, seminary training would expose their secrets and bring into the open the humans behind so much of what churches chalk up to mystery and spiritual force.

I was discovering a greater openness to critique as not a challenge to my faith but as necessary to develop a faith worth having. Critiques of my religious tradition at Columbia threw me a bit. At Harvard, it wasn't so frightening. Class readings and after-class conversations that spilled into local coffee shops gave me a better sense of other perspectives and opinions. These meetings in coffee shops were freeing. I was energized talking about new ideas and new takes on old ideas.

I was losing my evangelical edge, and at times I was embarrassed to think I'd once been so narrow and parochial in my attitudes. This, however, wasn't something I shared with Fred and Barbara Lucas, my mother, or people from my religious communities back in Buffalo or New York.

Despite the challenges to my sense of faith, there were traditional markers of religious community at Harvard. It had a long legacy from the Divinity School old chapel in Divinity Hall, where Ralph Waldo Emerson famously urged those listening to "acquaint thyself with divinity first hand," and where great preachers like Charles Adams had honed their craft on campus. Yet it was first and foremost a place where hard questions were asked and faith either withstood the challenge or didn't. For some of the faculty and many of the students, as far as I could tell, there was nothing personal at stake. This wasn't the case for me. I was still thinking about the church and my role within it.

Something like once a year, Reverend Lucas invited me back to preach, and my evolving perspectives changed my preaching. I gave less attention to personal salvation and less attention to God breaking into human history and making things happen. My sermons were less emotion driven, and I found it increasingly difficult to tell people what God would do for them if they were righteous. Ethics and morals were shifting me away from static notions carved out of scripture without any consideration to the historical and cultural context of the biblical world. The Exodus wasn't about poor people in the United States. The story of Job said nothing about God's plan to give oppressed blacks economic relief. Before divinity school, I handled context through a quick turn to the *Interpreter's Bible* and commentaries looking for a few key ideas that I could use to introduce the meaning of scripture before applying it to the contemporary lives of God's people. Now it was different.

Like the theologians I read in school, I preached human accountability and human responsibility. And I told stories about Jesus the Christ for what they said of his ministry and what those lessons might tell us about our own ethical responsibilities. It was hard to fit this perspective into church settings, where it was all about personal salvation and the signs of that salvation: the right way to dress, the right way to walk and talk, the right way to praise the Lord. Every dimension of life was monitored through this concern for personal salvation as the last best thing churches could provide. But I no longer cared if people came forward after the sermon to give their life to Christ. Rather than telling people to come to the altar and get their hearts right with God, I'd invite them to join the church and partner to change the world.

While I'd found it increasingly difficult to participate in services as I moved toward the completion of my undergraduate degree, going back to give these sermons wasn't so challenging. I felt more in control now. It was me, fully present and talking to the people, using my limited insights to take them into the biblical world. My sermons weren't looking for magic in scriptural accounts; rather I wanted to unpack ethical and moral codes to apply within our circumstances. I wasn't waiting on the Lord to give me the words to say; I controlled that time in the pulpit. There was no blank page for the Holy Spirit to fill.

The people in the pews felt the change. Fewer people came forward than in my earlier days, and I imagined some wondered to themselves what Harvard was doing to me. I, on the other hand, felt I was finally doing it right. This shift in my preaching was a victory for me but didn't get the job done from the perspective of traditional ministry. So, in time, invitations to head back to Brooklyn to preach dried up.

This didn't hurt or offend me. I could see that for some my sermons were probably a bit dry, without the same energy and passion as others exhibited, without the proclamation of a risen Lord made with wild body movement and lots of sweat dripping from my face. I didn't "whoop" before, but I did get a little loud and a bit animated. Now my sermons were more subdued.

I was okay with all this because for me it reflected intellectual and spiritual growth. I was finding what I'd left New York to discover.

Chapter Ten

THE CHURCH ACROSS FROM THE PARK

At the time I attended Harvard, each Master of Divinity student was required to do "field education" as part of their course of study. For two of the three years in the program, we worked for a nonprofit organization, or a church, with the goal of linking classroom experience with more practical vocational training.

I approached the pastor of one of the local AME churches about doing my field education at his church. He told me there were already a good number of students completing their requirements there, and so there would be little for me to do other than sit in the pulpit and read scripture. I'd already done that at Agape and Bridge Street. I wanted something more challenging at Harvard, so I decided to go to Grant AME Church, which was smaller and less overrun with student ministers. Fred Lucas vouched for the pastor there and suggested it could be a good fit for me.

Reverend Roland McCall said the church couldn't pay me. I was fine with that because the position wasn't about the money, as I had fellowships that covered my expenses. On top of my financial aid, I had know-how: figuring out ways to pay bills and make ends meet was something I was good at. In place of payment, McCall promised there would be opportunities for me to get involved, including preaching. I didn't have a good sense of what I was going to get out of it, although I was certain I needed more than I'd gotten at Agape and Bridge Street. I was already a preacher with some experience in a church setting. I thought I had a handle on the basic requirements of what it took to be a minister. I knew how to preach, perform wedding ceremonies, conduct funerals, lead Bible studies, and organize youth programs. But I'd been sheltered from many of the tedious tasks that went along with the pastorate—church reports, budgets, and so on. Working at Grant Church wouldn't keep me from the less glamorous dimensions of ministry, and there could be some benefit to that.

If I am honest, snobbery about church status informed my take on field education and on my placement at Grant Church. I'd worked at Bridge Street with one of the stars of the denomination, and I was already dealing with some major theological changes that started in New York and took the shape of hard questions: Does ministry really meet perceived needs? Does faith really address suffering? What do ministers actually offer in exchange for the financial and emotional support they receive? I'd come from a large and impressive church in New York, and I was wrestling with my faith. What could Grant offer me? Working at Grant or anywhere else for that matter wouldn't have much impact on me, or so I thought.

Grant Church is in Roxbury, Massachusetts—at that time, a somewhat economically challenged area and home to a significant African American population. As a physical structure, Grant didn't stand out. It wasn't imposing in that sense. It didn't demand aesthetic attention, and one could easily drive down the relatively busy street and give the church little attention and consideration. It fit into its surroundings.

In terms of size, Grant was about the same as Agape, a few hundred members with a similar economic background, a similar commitment to energetic worship, and the same basic doctrines and creeds. Grant, Agape, and Bridge Street used the same *Book of Discipline* as a guide, although there was room to tailor its requirements to the culture of the particular church. Churches could rearrange the order of service a bit or downplay some of the denominational regulations about low-level leadership positions. Like Bridge Street Church, the membership came from various locations—some came from the north and some were in Boston because members of their families at some point moved from southern communities in search of economic opportunities and greater social space.

When I started working at Grant, I had more potential than proven ability as a pastor. But even at that stage, there were certain perks and privileges I'd become accustomed to and that I wanted to maintain.

At Bridge Street I was accustomed to someone on staff—typically a volunteer—taking care of the less spiritually driven dimensions of ministry. Outside the church, few successful businesses rely on a willing heart rather than expertise when giving people responsibilities and assignments. But the churches I'd worked at did precisely this because on both the religious and the administrative levels, churches tend to favor the leading of the Lord (and God's ability to use anyone for God's glory) over formal training. Rather than securing the necessary skills and talents, they too often assume divine assistance will cover any shortcomings. God's desire for the progress of the church ultimately will override any human weaknesses, or so they prayerfully assume. The volunteer culture of churches combined with the sense of calling (and perhaps some formal training) that framed ministry made the preacher a special breed.

Recognition of this special status could involve simple things like ministers not paying for anything when in the company of church members, or having people—"armor bearers"—in place who serve as personal assistants and who serve God through service to the minister of God by driving the preacher around, maintaining the preacher's robes, running errands for the minister, and so on. This is considered a position of honor because the armor bearer is in direct contact with the anointed preacher. Sometimes people just fell into this role, particularly, it seemed to me, when a church friend might begin informally accompanying a young minister to speaking engagements, driving him around, collecting his robe, and so on.

The small ministerial staff had more responsibilities than I had at Agape or Bridge Street. As one of two youth ministers, I helped compile the financial and activity reports we presented to the presiding elder. I'd never done that type of paperwork at my other churches. My previous experience was more limited; I'd paid little attention to the mechanics of ministry: budgets, and the like. How these churches worked hadn't been in my purview. And now I had to figure it out in real time.

This behind-the-scenes work wasn't anything I enjoyed. It was the unrecognized labor finished in the office with no one cheering, no one impressed—the nuts-and-bolts workings of the institutional church that weren't memorable.

There were benefits to being at Grant, like new friends who attended the church but lived near me in Cambridge. We'd get together on Fridays and relax, play video games, watch movies, and talk. We shared stories about our personal lives. But our church talk and church gossip didn't have the same level of intimacy. Talk about my personal life included some messiness (sanitized a bit, of course), but it seemed to me I would be letting them down by telling them about my questions and theological anxieties. Despite everything, I was supposed to have a better grip on religious life than that. I couldn't share my theological weaknesses with them, and I couldn't talk to the other young minister on staff. On some level we were ministerial rivals, competing for a limited number of high-profile opportunities in the church and at least passively arranging a pecking order on the ministerial staff.

You would think if God calls all these people for the same purpose, to minister to God's people, there would be no need for a pecking order. We might have our own spiritual gifts, but we would be equals. The calling would make them of equal value within the ministry, at least in (theological) theory. Then again, this type of thinking runs contrary to what I and every other Christian knew. Everyone has particular talents and skills given by God, but those talents and skills aren't equal. Some were valued more than others; some provided opportunity for more visibility than others. If you preached with passion and caught the attention of the congregation, you'd get more exposure to key opportunities—monetary offerings and other tangible and intangible perks—than if you were, say, a good counselor.

The desire for recognition could make ministers do some ungenerous and backhanded things. Who do you think generated so many of the rumors and the gossip? So it was important to be careful with what you said and to whom you said it. Information turned into gossip, and that stuff spread quickly in the church. An ill-conceived comment could cause a world of hurt and embarrassment. I had learned to be cautious and careful with information, and that training kept me from telling anyone too much.

I'd seen and heard about too many ministers and other church leaders— particularly during testimony services when people shared their spiritual battles, shortcomings, and triumphs—share a personal failure (like drinking, smoking, adultery, fornication). What they thought was a moment of spiritual victory turned out to be a "mark" on their record, resulting in fewer ministerial responsibilities and a professional setback. This wasn't going to happen to me.

Only I knew the full story of my life. Say just enough, and load it with the right catchphrases and paraphrases of scripture and the occasional "God is good, and I'm blessed." This phrase served to redirect the comment and to put the situation on God, which lessened its negative impact. There was a performative element to this process, and everyone had a part. I'd make that kind of general "say nothing" statement, and in response, the questioner would affirm my faith with a similarly generic statement—"Yes, God is!"—followed by a smile, handshake, or hug.

Each ordained preacher at Grant and everywhere else had convinced church leadership of his or her calling or removed enough doubt to make the church community comfortable with the idea of that person being a minister. I'd gone through all of this at Agape, and then Bridge Street, and now at Grant. The people at Grant did what most African American Christians do with new a member of the staff: they welcomed me.

I worked with young people, often taking a few of them to the Harvard Law School gym on Saturday to play basketball and talk over a lunch of Chinese food. And I worked with the other youth minister to plan events—a fashion show to raise money, a party for young members.

Many of the kids with whom I worked had similar backgrounds to those I'd worked with in New York. They'd faced tragedy and knew too many people who had died young. Their schools and social circles could present challenges to the teachings the church tried to instill in them, and parents were aware of this predicament. Boston wasn't a war zone, but life was fragile and couldn't always be protected from damage and demise. Even places like the playground across from the church, which should have been a problem-free zone, was often the site of shady activities.

I imagine this playground was built to be a place where young people in the neighborhood could experience the outdoors, exercise, and enjoy life. It was one of the few spaces available for such activities in an area marked by decay and city housing developments. But by the time I had arrived, it also had a reputation for other activities, like drug deals. Regardless, the kids in the neighborhood adjusted, made the most of it, and were relatively safe as long as they knew whom to look out for, knew the signs of trouble about to happen, and had the strength to say no to offers coming their way.

Every Sunday on my way to Grant, I saw that playground. Despite some forgetfulness and cloudy details that come with memories over twenty years old, I remember how the playground made me feel: uncomfortable. I avoided walking through it whenever I could. I felt out of place there, vulnerable and unable to control what took place there the way I could at the church. It was a symbol of something my faith couldn't harness but that continually confronted me. Thinking about my work as a Grant youth minister kept the playground and its dangers in the forefront of my mind.

Parents assumed I could get through to their children, even though I represented perhaps a higher level of authority than they did. Even so, parents reasoned, I was a young man and seemed to have some sense of the music their kids liked and the language they spoke. So when parents recognized that gang activity and drug deals were getting too close to home, they'd contact me to talk with their children, to pray for their children, and to offer a bit of comfort and assurance that God would make a way. These young people listened politely as I talked.

Despite expectations, and a few more years of ministry under my belt, I wasn't prepared to offer these parents or their children anything that was substantive—just a few words, a Bible lesson, and a prayer. I wore the robe and had the title—"Reverend"—but . . . I had questions and concerns that I tried to hide. If what I'd believed about the Christian faith wasn't a lie, a misstatement of human life, and a need meant to control people rather than help them, it was overly optimistic and based on a wish rather than being grounded in anything verifiable. I couldn't say any of this, so I'd do what I was asked to do. But I resented queries from church members for good answers. In their requests for help was the assumption that I had access to special knowledge and that I could do or say something that would make a difference. I was going through the motions in my youth programming, counseling, and preaching.

In the pulpit, the pastor instructed me to let the people get happy with me during my sermons, to give them a reason to get up on Monday. In other words, I should whoop—raise my voice with a matching intensity in the rhythmic flow of my words, jerking and jumping about the pulpit. But that wasn't me, and I didn't see a good reason for that type of joy and energy anyway. In sermons, Bible studies, youth meetings, and other church activities, we talked about the power and compassion of God, but it seemed rather empty when street violence and despair were taking away our people. Too many members of the church knew personally the young people who were dying because of the kind of activities that playground represented for me. And my sermons had little to say about the situation beyond empty clichés and passages of scripture forced into a contemporary context. I gave members of the church opportunities to pray about life challenges. I gave them short-term relief from their problems—a chance to catch their breath. The walls of Grant provided a space away from the playground. For those who commuted to the church from some distance, what I offered might be enough. They saw the playground and its activities but drove away able to say, "If not but for the grace of God, there go I."

For those who lived near Grant, after church service they were on their own. The words of wisdom I and other ministers offered and the feeling of relief from the prayers gave way. And faith's inability to meet needs surfaced with full force in the intersections of that playground and the church pulpit.

The feeling that I had little to offer people in my role as minister was reinforced every time I saw that playground or heard about a tragedy involving one of the kids from the church or one of the neighborhood kids who came around the church on occasion. My theology seemed inadequate for the task, and my sermons, prayers, counseling, and bible teachings were built upon a faith I was questioning.

The issues for me were growing more intense, and while there was only so much I could say about them in church, I used seminar papers or class assignments as an opportunity to wrestle with them.

While in New York I'd moved away from strict evangelical thinking to a more liberal perspective, but in Boston even that was proving insufficient. I still believed in God, but I was starting to give greater attention to what moral evil—the pain and suffering experienced by communities—told us about the truth of the gospel message: What can we say about God from our vantage point of human history and human experience? What does it mean to be a Christian within the contemporary world, still marked by so many forms of injustice and discrimination? Was the Bible something special, a unique receptacle for cosmic wisdom instead of just a piece of literature like other collections of stories?

Christ still mattered to me, but I was thinking about the ministry of Jesus—what he did with and for people as opposed to the dramatic story of death and resurrection. I would never have been able to wrap my mind around this issue back in Buffalo because I was too tied to notions of hellfire and an angry God.

I started thinking about theology only in relationship to what it could tell us about the world and how to reenvision and improve the world. I gave almost no consideration to the Holy Spirit at this point, and sin moved from personal misconduct to collective wrongdoing: racism, sexism, classism, and homophobia. No thinking about heaven and hell, just the material world occupied by living creatures. This world is all we could know. Praxis, not prayer, had significant impact on the material and psychological quality of life.

Did my presence in the church, and in the world as a representative of the church, mean anything that mattered at all?

Perhaps ministers at our best were more like community organizers—providing space and questions that helped people discover themselves and their capacity to effect change? That might be the case, but it wasn't a way of thinking that would find much support in black churches: "If that's all that our pastor can do for us, what makes the pastor special? If the pastor doesn't know any more than we do, what's the point in having a pastor?" Church members might think these things and might even voice them in soft tones, but as long as the minister preaches in a convincing way and handles the other spiritual dimensions of church life, these whispered questions had limited consequence.

So much that had concerned me in my evangelical days seemed of no significance now. Issues of spiritual growth began to feel superficial at best, as if

I'd been preoccupied with the look, the external stuff of human life as opposed to its real content. All show and no substance was another way I was beginning to think about so much of my spiritual life and ministerial activities.

The realities I encountered outside the church ripped away at my theology and faith, and a compromise was required if I was going to be able to hold onto even a piece of them. There were lots of contradictions and inconsistencies in my thinking and in my faith claims, but this was all part of a process of growth. It was interesting and powerful stuff, but it didn't exactly provide me with good material for sermons.

Church members were polite, but I knew my preaching was neither inspired nor inspiring. My work at Grant was an act and not much more. In my performances, I tried to make scripture speak to contemporary need, but I was finding scripture lacking when it came to issues of gender, sexuality, class, and slavery. I was beginning to see both my use of scripture and the church's reliance on it as problematic: borrowing the fantastic stories dreamed up by others. Trying to make these stories fit contemporary life required a lot of stretching, manipulation, and forgetting of facts—historical and scientific facts. Other stories and sources were needed, so I began turning my attention to African American literature, the arts, and other forms of culture to find more relevant ways to understand the misery and mystery of life.

I had a different way of assessing the "good" life as well, and all this was making it difficult to see the value in the traditional—"This is the way we've always done it"—talk and activities of churches.

I was a Christian, but I was becoming a different type of Christian: one concerned with the world as it is and with what we are able to achieve within the world.

In New York my religion had become *liberal* and bent toward a progressive agenda; in Boston it was becoming Liberal with a capital *L*. I was putting the welfare of people above the preservation of religious tradition. Could I say I had a calling to help people and give little attention to the look, smells, sounds, tastes, and feel of life? My old evangelical religion had made me afraid of life, had made me believe that experiencing life would cost me my soul. I was unlearning this.

Harvard faculty like my adviser, Gordon Kaufman, and other key professors responsible for my academic growth—Richard R. Niebuhr and Margaret Miles—showed me a way of thinking about my faith by reflecting on how religion had performed in the past. They helped me see its connections to our cultural worlds and the intersections of religion and the contemporary challenges facing the nation in which I lived. Their lectures, discussions, and casual comments pushed me to appreciate the cultural dimensions of religion and the material nature of faith. Through a turn to the visual arts, literature, film, and other signs and symbols of humans making sense of their world, I found a different grounding for religion.

Chapter Eleven

GODLESS

I was learning the language of the professional theologian, and I used it awkwardly at first. I'd practice its vocabulary with friends at coffee shops or just walking around. I'd throw around a bit of jargon here and a bit of jargon there, and I'd pepper it with a reference to this thinker or that thinker.

I spent time thinking about a variety of theological issues meant to get at the questions I'd been asking myself: the nature of moral evil, who Jesus was and is for the Christian community (Christology), the end times (eschatology), the nature and purpose of the Church (ecclesiology), and a variety of others that made up theological thinking over the centuries. But of all these, doctrine of God was the major concern for me because it seemed all my issues and questions were connected to ideas of God and what God does.

God was no longer the dominating and awe-inspiring cosmic force I'd come to love (and fear) as a young born-again Christian in Buffalo. God created problems and then punished humans for falling prey to those problems. I had been taught that God loved people and worked for our welfare, bringing faithful people the possibility of redemption and righteousness. But all that seemed to be so much talk and nothing more.

I was done with that God, the harsh and judgmental God that came across as something of a mean-spirited and sadistic bastard that you couldn't even complain about under your breath without opening a can of cosmic "whoop-ass."

No more superstition and no more supernatural ideas clogging my mind and restricting me. No gods to fear, to pray to, and to wait on.

I was no longer hamstrung by the moods and mysterious logic of a cosmic force responsible for all things. There was something comforting in this rethinking of God from this larger-than-life *BEING* to a partner with humanity whose power was limited and confined, even if this limitation was self-imposed.

My new God was still loving and just, but without power to make anything happen. Gone was the forceful God that terrorized me and was now replaced with one that could only attempt to persuade people to do the right thing. It was that "still, small voice" my mother talked about when she was waiting on the Lord to tell her something. This more vulnerable deity was easier to approach, less moody, and more sympathetic to human frailty.

The death of the powerful cosmic "father" was freeing. It had been a vengeful, so very difficult to please, and so easily offended God that I constantly wondered if I was doing something wrong. I'd regularly assumed that I'd sinned in "thought, word, or deed." Everything about me as a human opened me to that God's displeasure and disappointment. It couldn't be otherwise, considering the impossible standards set by this God and humanity's inability to complete tasks that don't revolve around their own selfish needs and desires.

Ministers were expected to have their lives under control. In light of that, my sins were even more disappointing to God, who had special goals and plans for people like me. My failure to fulfill these goals really disappointed laity, who were well aware of them, and could even cause weak Christians to backslide: "See, I told you there was nothing to this faith. That church thing is nothing but a racket, and that preacher is no better than any other hustler!" So much mental energy and physical restraint went into avoiding falling into that trap.

My shift away from a very demanding God softened the fall. Not everything I had once frowned on was actually so very bad. Just because things brought joy and happiness to people didn't make them problematic. No need anymore for some version of an ascetic life. Not everything was a hanging offense, not like before. I dropped the idea of original sin and its backstory about a cosmic creation. I felt like I was finally catching my breath after holding it for years.

I enjoyed my life more because there was more I could do without staggering guilt, without constantly wondering if I would still merit entrance to heaven. Clubs on Saturday, bars with friends, the occasional curse-laced tirade, and the list goes on.

This didn't mean life without limits, and it didn't mean I could do anything I wanted. Losing that demanding God didn't mean I lost my moral compass and my ethics. It simply meant my ethics and morality came from human sources as opposed to coming from a phantom figure and its magical book.

This shift away from that biblical God of vengeance to a friendly version came with an evolving perspective on issues such as sexuality, sexism, classism, and homophobia. Nothing even resembling biblical social codes was relevant. And without those nonsensical dictates—so difficult to preach, but ministers try—justification for brutal behavior went out the window.

We are screwed-up animals, self-aware, communicative, and evolving. Our existence is explained—to the extent it can be—through science, not through a bizarre story of creation with some dirt, a rib, and some magic words. I was becoming increasingly comfortable with much of what had been attributed to God and other forces really being the result of biology. When compared to the wizardry of the Bible, this might not seem such a fantastic accounting of humanity, but this understanding instilled in me a sense of awe, a sense of wonder based on how unlikely our existence really is in light of everything that had to line up in order to make it happen. Our presence on Earth isn't the same as a God speaking something into existence out of a void, but it is pretty spectacular—in a scientific kind of way. This take on life is harder to preach and does not allow the same opportunity to whoop, "In the beginning . . . Amen! Was the Big Bang! Hallelujah! The energy expanded out! Can I get an Amen?".

I took these ideas as far as I could at the Divinity School, and in my third year I began thinking about PhD applications. I worked on draft after draft of my admission statement. I had to get the tone and the content right. The faculty members reading it had to think, "Yes, this is the place for Pinn and we need to work with him." Letters of recommendation that spoke to my ability had to be secured, and that process started long before the actual request for letters was made. Smart comments in class and during office hours; insightful papers and exams all provided the groundwork for requesting an excellent letter.

I put work into these applications, mailed them off, and then I waited for replies—hoping things would work out for me.

I received letters of acceptance from several schools, and most people thought I'd go back to New York, to Union Theological Seminary and study with the "father" of black theology, James Cone. From that first conversation when I was a college student, he'd influenced my thinking, and I'd continued to read him as a master-level student—his work playing a role in my evolving sensibilities. Black theology and its aggressive and impassioned commitment to social justice, combined with the constructive theology tradition at Harvard carried out by Kaufman and Niebuhr, gave me some theological breathing space. And while Union made sense, there were also compelling reasons to stay at Harvard.

I didn't need to "learn" to do theology as an African American. Being an African American was a part of my sense of self and social identity. I understood that dimension of myself. What I didn't fully understand was the larger theological tradition and the study of religion with which it is associated. I could get that at Harvard, where I already understood the institutional politics and culture. I had enough on my intellectual plate that I didn't need the added task of figuring out how an institution worked before I could begin my next phase of study.

I decided to stay at Harvard. The school had its problems—the "If you are having difficulties, perhaps you don't belong here" attitude, the odd forms of competition between students, and so on—but I had a handle on those issues.

I'd ended my Master of Divinity program with this softer version of God and all the theological stuff that went along with it, and I was now in Harvard University's PhD program in the study of religion, still advised by Gordon Kaufman. Theology was my focus. It gave me a way to wrestle with the questions crowding my mind and exposed me to readings and arguments that sparked my imagination.

My work at Grant became increasingly difficult to continue. The church people I spent time with had issues that weren't resolved by my appeal to God—

any God with any power. And despite my efforts, I was left with a dilemma, a negative tension that couldn't be maintained. Moving between the classroom and the pulpit, did I offer people something that could stand up to scrutiny? In a backhanded way, I was really asking a more fundamental and vexing question: Does God exist? Of course this was the fundamental concern; why wouldn't it be, when so much of my theological reform had to do with God?

Everything rested on the answer to this question, no matter how liberal my Christianity had become. Does God exist?

It was a difficult question to ask, but to live and work based on a lie, and to convince others to live in accordance with that same lie, would be even more difficult. If the answer was no, if God didn't exist, all that God supported in my thinking and in my ethics would fall apart. It would mean I had spent years bending myself to the will of an illusion and working to bring others in line with my delusional thinking. If God didn't exist, I was no better than those who took advantage of human need and gave people "snake oil" when they needed surgery.

Was God present in the world in a knowable way, in a manner demonstrating concern with the conditions of life? Nothing about the traumas of human existence, the sad realities in that playground across from Grant Church, and the continuation of oppression suggested God was present and concerned—certainly not a God worth all that the ministry required of me.

Or perhaps, I reasoned, God's presence is found in the nastiness of life? Maybe God is found in the injustice in the world? That was a radical idea for me, but even that possibility didn't satisfy. It wasn't that I couldn't stand the idea of a God who isn't good and compassionate but instead is the source of misery and pain. Even this idea of God lacked the evidence I needed. There was no sign, no real indicator that the pain and suffering encountered had a depth and tenacity that couldn't be accounted for through human will and idiosyncrasies. Just as the good in the world was easily explained through the efforts of humans, so was the nasty shit. Everything pointed back to human activity in the world, without any appeal to extra-human forces at work in the world.

With a greater sense of ease than I would have anticipated, I said it: *There is no God.*

I'd finally reached the point where there was no alternative. The world is as it is, and religion is what it is—flawed and incomplete, without the ability to resolve pressing historical problems because it is based on an illusion and a mythical figure.

It wasn't that God was dead. This would have assumed God had been at some point alive, somehow present and "real." My conclusion was more fundamental than that: God never existed but has always been nothing more than a symbol, a piece of language and culture constructed by humans. To say God is dead, for me, would have been the equivalent of saying that language dies, that words die rather than simply falling out of use.

No God or gods.

Once I could no longer find a way to theologically maintain God and hold onto the significance of my historical moment, letting go of God was natural.

Starting at Columbia, moving through the Master of Divinity program to the PhD program, I'd changed.

The exact day I made this statement is no longer fresh in my mind. Marking that particular moment out, placing it on a calendar to celebrate each year was never important to me. More important was the freedom and obligation it placed on me. That "being" I'd worshipped for so many years turned out to be a component of my imagination, a way to cover my insecurities and uncertainties.

"God" was a useless piece of human language. I knew some people believed God and Nature were one in the same, which allowed them to move away from a personal God, but I didn't see the point in using the term *God* at all. Why cloud the issue? Why misname Nature when it was just as easy to call it what it is: Nature? God was gone, and would be referenced only as a negative lesson, but without any pretense to there being anything behind the term.

I'd outgrown the term *God*. It no longer meant anything to me; I'd finally seen how empty it is and for how long I'd invested a piece of vocabulary with influence that actually belonged to humans. Considering how strong my belief in God had been, this final push away from belief in God was surprisingly easy. And it didn't involve a long period of anger over having been duped for so many years. There was confusion on the part of others over my move, but for me it was rather straightforward.

Image 10. The author in his Cambridge apartment after receiving the Master of Divinity degree from Harvard Divinity School.

*   *   *

As I was growing up, "What would I be without the Lord on my side?" was a common question for people in my church family. I now see that it spoke to a desperate effort to avoid being on our own. Theists need God to fill the void, to provide a cushion against the world. I let go of this fear, and it raised questions: "How could you let go of God and continue to go on?" "How could it be so easy?"

People who've heard some of my story ask these questions assuming that the loss of God is also the loss of any reason to live. Surely it wouldn't be possible to live a moral and ethical life without the cosmic cop holding us in check. My rejection of the idea of God didn't reduce my sense of life but rather enlarged it. I was now in direct contact with living creatures fundamentally responsible for their quality of life. There was no buffer—God—between us.

I did not feel lost as a consequence of this decision, and I didn't feel like I'd lost anything substantive; it was much like a child letting go of Santa Claus or the Easter Bunny.

"You must be angry with God . . . an unanswered prayer, your mother's illness." This was another response to my statement of disbelief. If they could make it personal, an angry reaction, questionable wants and desires, they could keep God safe. Then the problem would be with my response to suffering, with my demand for material comfort, and my assumption that things could be worked out through reason. If it were personal, they'd have me "between a rock and a hard place." They'd keep God on the throne, and I'd look like a petty fool without adequate faith.

My response to this has always been the same. Despite what some wanted to believe, nothing about this decision had to do with personal disappointment. I didn't reject the idea of God because I'd prayed for something and didn't get it or because life had thrown me a curveball. If it was about personal disappointment, I would never have joined the church and accepted Jesus the Christ as my personal savior. My mother's poor health and my parents' deteriorating relationship would have been enough pain and disappointment to keep me away.

It wasn't about me and my personal wants.

I rejected God because the concept of God had no demonstrated ability to help *people* based on where they are and in light of the issues with which they wrestle. It was found wanting and empty—and it had to go. I valued the integrity of material life above the fantasies and ghosts found in the church.

There was a period of overlap during which I was a nontheist with a church affiliation, with decreased responsibilities and infrequent appearances at church, but still holding the title of Reverend. It was uncomfortable trying to be true to my new way of thinking while maintaining membership in the church.

I don't remember exactly how long this overlap was or what my reasoning was for it. I didn't doubt my new thinking, but maybe I was struggling to put in words the decisions I'd reached. Perhaps it was an interest in the people, despite their concern for God. I don't know why, but it couldn't last. I couldn't remain in the church. I couldn't be in the pulpit preaching what I no longer believed. I couldn't pray to a God that didn't exist. I couldn't and wouldn't ask people in need of help to participate in their own dehumanization through church rituals, creeds, and doctrines.

Maintaining my ordination and church membership would make me a hypocrite, and I wouldn't hold that title—"Reverend Hypocrite, pastor of the Church of Gotta Get Paid."

I had to make a break. I had to surrender my ordination. That was key!

So I contacted the pastor and informed him that I would no longer be serving on the ministerial staff. I don't recall his response, but it wouldn't have mattered to me anyway. There was nothing he or anyone else could have said or done that would have changed my mind.

Contacting the pastor took care of one layer of church authority. Since I had been ordained by one of the church's bishops, surrendering ordination would require contacting my bishop with the news. So I wrote to my bishop indicating that I was surrendering my ordination and would no longer function in a ministerial capacity. I stopped attending the annual conference of my region required of all ministers as a clear sign of my movement beyond the church.

I've been told the secretary continued to call my name as part of the roll call. And when I didn't answer, people assumed school kept me from attending, although classes or schoolwork would have never been an acceptable reason for missing the conference. I think the fact that my name continued to be called meant that the bishop either hadn't bothered to read my letter or that my abandonment of the church was not acknowledged. Either way, it didn't matter. I was gone—out of the church—and I wasn't returning.

On occasion I might attend a service like I would attend any cultural activity—a concert, a movie, a ball game—but it held no real meaning for me. I might also attend for research sake to supplement the materials available in the library. But I would never return to the church as an act of repentance and I wouldn't again embrace its teachings.

News about my departure from the church and its beliefs spread slowly. There was little reaction from students with whom I was close; they had their own issues with the church. I told my mother, and she responded with a mother's love. She told me she thought it was a phase I was going through and that she prayed I would find my way back to the church; but even if I didn't, she loved me, was proud of me, and always would be.

I wasn't particularly close to my siblings at that point—the age differences and different geographies were a bit of a barrier for us—so I didn't say much to them about it, but my mother talked to all of us and was a source of information. I knew what was happening with my brother and sisters through my at least weekly calls with my mother, and I assumed she told them about me, including the news about my departure from the church. My extended family certainly learned through my mother. What they thought about it didn't matter to me. I wasn't close enough to them—with a few exceptions—for it to be a concern I'd want or need to address.

I didn't share much of this change with my Bridge Street family. I wasn't preaching at the church much anymore, and my trips back to New York were rather restricted by time and money. Looking back on it, I'm not certain why I didn't reach out and share this major development with the people in Brooklyn I loved. I wasn't ashamed or embarrassed, or I would have kept it from my mother. Maybe I didn't want to hurt their feelings, to have them question what they had done for me. I don't know.

Reverends Fred and Barbara Lucas (Barbara had entered the ministry in Buffalo, at Agape) would have had a clue in that I no longer showed for the annual conference. They are too smart to have let this situation go past without some suspicion, but nothing was ever said to me that encouraged me to share my outlook.

It would be a good number of years before Fred and Barbara and I had anything resembling a conversation about my atheism and what they'd taught me to love about the Christian faith. I don't have much of a connection to Fred at this point—not because of my atheism, I don't think, but I am in contact with Barbara and the kids: Kemba, Hakim, and Kareem. My atheism is a running joke with the kids, but it isn't much of a topic of conversation with Barbara. She still prays for me, says, "God bless you" and includes me in her general religious conversation as if little about my theological orientation has changed. That's fine with me.

This is the tack taken by a variety of people with whom I am close. They are still in the church and they use with me the language of theism and the practices of theism meant to demonstrate love and concern: "God bless you" or "I'm praying for you." I don't take these expressions as insults or rejections of my atheism but rather as signs of appreciation from people who are including me in the ways they know. This, of course, isn't the case with everyone, but those situations I handle on a case-by-case basis.

I'd broken away from something, but I had no replacement. I didn't have an alternate community.

I had a sense of how humanism and atheism developed in African American communities, and I could trace them from slavery to the contemporary moment. I understood myself as part of a long-standing community of African American humanists, atheists, and freethinkers stretching from the early presence of enslaved Africans to that point in the twentieth century. But in terms of a practical community in my particular location, I wasn't certain where to go. What little I knew of humanist associations—and it wasn't much at all—tended to revolve around white Americans.

This perspective was new to me, and so I wasn't aware of a humanist or atheist community with which I could replace my church family. I'd heard about the Unitarian Universalist Association through students on the Harvard campus, but it seemed rather thin to me and somewhat weak on issues of race. The sense of ritual, at least as I gathered from students, wasn't going to be compelling for me either. And I knew nothing of the Ethical Culture Society.

I wasn't certain where to go in terms of relationships with the like-minded, but being able to reject what didn't work was a major accomplishment, and I was content.

I didn't discuss my departure from the church with faculty. Having personal conversations with faculty wasn't something I did with respect to any issue; rather, I expressed philosophically and theologically my changed mind through my work, from course work through the writing of my dissertation.

Chapter Twelve

THINKING MY THOUGHTS . . . YOU DON'T HAVE TO AGREE

I'm certain I talked too much about my dissertation, but people humored me. I was like most graduate students; I'd survived language training; made it through course work; completed a grueling set of qualifying examinations and the mental/emotional stress that went along with studying for them; and now, I was at the final stage—what the program was all about: the dissertation.

In lots of ways I was still shy—attempting to avoid social situations with people I didn't know well because small talk was torture. Yet when it came to my dissertation and its argument, I was aggressive and outspoken.

I'd been pretty quiet in classes until I'd force myself to make some comments to be noticed by the professor in preparation for PhD applications and then as a PhD student to prove I belonged. But when it came to my dissertation and questions about my academic plans stemming from the dissertation, not so much. It wasn't like I was sitting at my computer or walking across the campus when it hit me: "I've got a lot to say about this theology stuff and people better listen!" No, it developed slowly. Slow enough that I can't mark out a clear transition, a pronounced time when I was shy about announcing the end of God and the beginning of a new type of humanity.

With every opportunity to work it into conversation, I told people about the problematic tradition of redemptive suffering arguments within African American religious thought. Always animated and a bit loud, I went on about the way this thinking made a virtue of suffering and resulted in limited opportunities for sustained activism that might produce long-lasting results.

This sense of suffering as redemptive, I argued, was required by the dominant notion of God within black churches. How can God-based ways of thinking and doing produce the liberation advocates of God claim to desire? Whether or not I was asked to say more, I'd elaborate: People mattered more than this tradition of theodicy—a way of explaining God in light of human suffering. The solution was a rejection of God and an embrace of humanism as a more viable way of thinking about the struggle against oppression, a more viable way of creating a meaningful life for individuals and communities. I was following on the heels of other thinkers in providing a theological and religious advancement of humanism as the answer to human suffering and the tangled mess of talk about God and an effort to move through the world in light of rather odd demands associated with this idea of God. This work excited me, and I wanted to protect my ideas.

I've always been a bit OCD—although never diagnosed by a doctor, I have my rituals of checking doors, lights, and so on—and so going over things more than once, checking things in a ritualized way carried over to my dissertation. Leaving it unprotected in my small apartment wasn't an option. The door wasn't that secure, and if tested, it would have only kept lazy thieves out. To be safe, I kept the project more secure by carrying the disk in my backpack. (I'd only started using a computer, although I'd had one for a couple of years.) It was with me at all times. And I gave two of my most trusted friends— Benjamin Valentin and Nisé Nekheba—a copy of the disk to keep in their homes for extra safety. This was hard for me because it meant trusting people with my most important thoughts.

But I'd heard too many horror stories about corrupt disks and broken computers to feel safe just having extra disks in place. So, despite the limited likelihood that all the disks would end up corrupted or in some other way compromised, I also kept a hard copy of the dissertation in my freezer wrapped securely in plastic. It was the perfect location because refrigerator-freezers don't burn, and so if there had been a fire, the manuscript would have survived. And on top of all that, thieves were unlikely to take the time to go through the messy freezer in search of riches. I had it all thought out: back up plans for my dissertation chapters and backup plans for my backup plans.

When I recount what I went through to protect my dissertation, people listening generally think I went too far. But it wasn't just about keeping it safe. Everything took second place. Relationships and friendships could come and go (and they often did without much fanfare during my schooling), but that project was consistently in the front of my mind.

Like most people working on a dissertation they really care about—as opposed to simply putting something on paper to get out of the program—I was obsessed with it. To say it was important to me is an understatement. It wasn't just some words on pages sufficient to get me a degree and possibly a job. And while I hoped it would be published someday, it wasn't even the idea of having a book on a shelf with my name across the spine that motivated me and made that manuscript so important. This project shadowed my life, my intellectual and religious movement. My thoughts, my energy, my money were all poured into it. Nothing else mattered as much to me as completing it in a way that would help me and others think differently and more productively about religion, theology, and human suffering.

I'd been warned by some academics and friends not to write this project. "It will cause you more trouble within the profession than it is worth," they warned. "Write something that isn't so controversial," was their counsel. However, I had to write it. In a way, it wiped out all the sermons I'd given, set the record straight, and put things together for me.

Although it had no relationship to what would emerge as the "New Atheism," my project, I imagine, came across to some as a form of atheistic evangelism, a type of nontheistic fundamentalism. There was passion between those pages, but my goal was to present humanism as a better way to address injustice without having to embrace suffering.

It was both a personal and an academic study. It was personal because it helped to resolve my long-standing issues. I had left the church, but I was struggling to think about and talk about humanism in a way that allowed it to fill the space left by theism. This involved thinking about humanism as having the capacity to function like a religion, such was my immediate need—something to replace theism as my life compass. Humanism had to be both a way of interpreting experience and also a way of being in the world, of living and thinking. It was academic in that it brought me into conversation and allowed me to reformulate thought and knowledge on what was for me a vital topic.

Teaching and researching within a university or college system would allow me to continue the type of work started as a graduate student. I could have open questions, push for clear thinking without the same pretense to all the answers required of the minister. The classroom would be the best place for this type of work, and I'd write articles and hopefully books that would add new dimensions of thought to the nature and meaning of religion. I had experienced life as a minister, but being a professor—a teacher—was what I wanted, yet it was also something with which I was deeply unfamiliar.

I had to test this out. What would it be like to teach, to be responsible for a classroom? I worked out an answer by looking for opportunities to teach. I contacted Gordon-Conwell Theological Seminary and volunteered to teach a course: "You don't have to pay me; I would simply like an opportunity to offer a course. You can decide on the topic, and you can rest assured I will take seriously the responsibility."

The person with whom I spoke wasn't certain what to do with my offer. But, after more conversation, he agreed to let me teach a course on theodicy in the African American tradition. I was delighted, but I knew it would be a delicate situation in that I was a new humanist teaching a course on theodicy at a conservative Christian institution. From the very beginning of that course, I tried my best to bracket my perspective and keep to the materials. It wasn't particularly easy when, during the first meeting, a student asked me about my opinion on the topic and my personal religious position. I responded in a guarded fashion by reminding the student we needed to understand how the topic had been addressed across the years by a variety of figures and I didn't want to jump in with my opinion and mess up that process. I was proud of my ability to sidestep the question, but I hadn't celebrated for long before another student looked at the syllabus and asked me when we would be reading the Bible because it was the book that really mattered on the subject.

I was annoyed by the question and the assumption, but what was left of my pastoral composure resurfaced. I smiled and gently said I was certain they could secure biblical perspectives on this topic outside the classroom. And so, during our time together, we needed to address perspectives and opinions with which they were less familiar. Again, I was impressed by my delicate response when I really wanted to scream, "Who gives a damn what the Bible says? The Bible and what it teaches are the problem in the first place. Don't be so blind!"

There were no major problems or controversies throughout the course. Although our discussions were loud and animated, others in the building got used to the sounds coming from my classroom. I have little reason to believe the students took much away from the class; they most likely continued to believe as they had the first day: "Jesus saves and the Bible is the answer . . ." Nothing about their comments on the readings or their discussion of my remarks suggested this material was pushing them to examine their theological beliefs and assumptions. But they were respectful and attentive, and the course went well enough for the school to end up paying me and inviting me to teach again. This time I was to teach a course on African American religious history at an off-campus location in Roxbury.

I also taught two courses—on the philosophy of race—at Suffolk University. I asked the students for their feedback early in the semester, and they requested a more relaxed environment, fewer lectures, and that I remove the suit and "loosen up." I did my best to accommodate them on this score, although I continue to prefer a suit to a pair of jeans. They were hardworking students, with less socioeconomic privilege than the students I'd encountered at Harvard when I'd worked there as a teaching assistant. They might not have been as gifted, but they brought to the classroom ease and familiarity with life outside the academy.

I enjoyed being in the classroom and thought it was a life I could live for a good number of years. But if being a professor involved teaching and research, I needed to sample both. So, in addition to teaching courses, I tackled the research component of professional life by giving conference papers at professional meetings. I based these papers on new ideas and beefed up assignments for seminars. Participating in these professional meetings meant a good deal of travel on a student's budget. But I managed.

The opportunity to share my ideas and receive feedback in a professional setting was refreshing. I didn't do much of anything on my dissertation during a roughly six-month period, but I learned a great deal about the profession—enough to know that it was for me. I met some interesting people, got a sense of academic politics as people made side comments about various papers, and I had an opportunity to network.

I wanted and needed to be in the academy; the life of the academic, the professor, was the life I wanted. Knowing that, I went back to my dissertation full time, working to get it done within a time frame that would get me out of Harvard as quickly as possible. I had gone there to get an education, not to become comfortable and just hang out. I wanted to get in and get out. And now that I knew the academy was for me, there was no reason to delay. I'd slowed down my dissertation work in order to experience a bit of professional life as an academic, and I liked it. So now it was time to get the dissertation written and defended so that I could enter professional life full time.

I treated work on my dissertation like a job—every day and on weekends. I camped out in the library, working, trying to make sense of the issue. Some of the research took me to other locations, like Boston University's archives. For the most part it was just me, the Harvard library system, and a wooden chair and table—followed by my studio apartment. The library was better; my apartment was a depressing place. There was wood paneling on the walls, an odd and old kitchen that was dark with lots of unusable space, and a tiny bathroom right next to the oven with a claw foot tub. I had a futon that served as a bed and couch, my "desk"—a board and two file cabinets on top of which sat my metal-cased IBM computer with the two floppy-disk drives—and some bookshelves.

My apartment was in a working-class neighborhood where I wasn't welcomed. My "neighbors" made that clear by telling me to go back where I belonged, making certain I had a hard time finding a parking spot, and calling the police and saying my car had been abandoned whenever I left town for any stretch of time. They even complained when I tried to learn to rollerblade. My landlord delivered the news: "They don't want to see you outside on those skates." Damn. It wasn't a home, but it was a place to get out of the rain and the snow. I didn't like the place, but I also had no intention on being there long-term. It was just a place to sleep, eat, and get work done.

I'd take my notes and write, and once I had a chapter drafted, I'd put it aside for a day or two, watch some television, chill for a little while, and then I'd edit it down to its proper content and length. I'd then hand it off to Professor Kaufman for feedback. He was generous with his time, and his feedback reached me in good order—handwritten in the margins and more comments at the end of the chapter. I'd make changes and start work on the next chapter. Once we'd completed the process, moving from chapter to chapter, he read the entire manuscript and offered a last round of feedback. I made revisions, and then let David Hall—the other Harvard Divinity School faculty member on my committee—read it. I received only minor suggestions from Hall. The revisions were made. A friend and I read over the entire manuscript, corrected typos, and so on, and made it ready for delivery to Kaufman, Hall, and Anthony Appiah, the third member of my committee (who was on the faculty in the Harvard Graduate School of Arts and Sciences from which I would receive the PhD).

Everything I could do had been done. I put in the paperwork for my defense, made the arrangements (with a great deal of assistance from Kaufman's secretary), and waited. I'd heard horror stories about people's projects not surviving the defense. Those cautionary tales were tough to hear, but I knew I'd done a good job and had already gotten positive feedback from most of the committee. Despite all this, however, when it was time to defend the dissertation, my committee shocked me.

I arrived at Kaufman's office in the library. The members of the committee, after shaking hands and greeting me, invited me to leave the office while they had a conversation. I thought it would be a brief time for them to figure out the order of the questions and to get a sense of the general thinking on my project. I was wrong.

I waited, walking about and wondering what was taking place in the office. Were they simply lost in conversation? Were they praising it, thinking of where and when it should be published? Were they talking about the brilliance of the project? Or were they ripping it apart, talking about how horrible and misguided the manuscript was and that it couldn't pass? Maybe they were going further and wondering how I'd even gotten into the program in the first place? I wasn't certain what to think—was the delay a good thing or a bad thing? It seemed like such a long time before the door opened, and, finally, I was invited back in.

Nervous doesn't begin to describe how I was feeling as I walked through the door. I shook hands with each of them again and took a seat. The three of them were on one side and I sat opposite them. The mood was somber as Kaufman looked at me, paused, and with what I remember as a stern look said, "There are problems . . ." There are problems? Problems?

I was thrown. I thought the project might need some revisions, some corrections, but nothing that would spark a "There are problems" conversation.

Things got intense. I fought for my project and pushed back as respectfully as I could. When it was all said and done, I learned that I had revisions to make on several of the chapters, and each member of the committee wanted to review the changes before the project would be considered defended, finished, and appropriate for the degree.

I got up to leave, hoping to go slowly enough to avoid awkwardness in the hallway with Hall and Appiah, but Kaufman stopped me and asked me to stay behind.

I braced myself, not knowing what he could possibly say at that point. But I knew I wasn't going to come across as weak, as not having the emotional strength and the intellectual ability to get through the program. I wouldn't be the sad story people told about the student who didn't make it. I wouldn't be the justification for not admitting someone else: "Well, Pinn seemed good as well. He had a degree from the Divinity School and a BA from Columbia, but he didn't make it through. I don't know that we should take a chance on this applicant . . ." That wasn't going to happen. I wouldn't be *that guy*.

Kaufman looked at me, paused, and told me there would be no shame in delaying the degree, completing revisions, and waiting until the next year to graduate. No one—and by this he meant himself—would think less of me if I took some time. There would be no negative assumptions concerning my abilities, at least from him. He was attempting to be compassionate from an academic point of view. This was generous, but I told him that I'd purchased a robe for commencement that I really couldn't afford and that my mother had her plane ticket. I would finish that year and do what was required to make that happen. Wait? For what? I was getting out of that place that summer. No one on that campus would have an opportunity to mock me because I didn't complete when I said I would. I was graduating. Period.

We shook hands, and I left the office. I was going to be done with that place even if it meant not sleeping again until after commencement. I'd get the work done and get that dissertation approved.

The last few weeks before finally getting approval on my dissertation were academic hell—limited sleep, lots of work, and an air of uncertainty about it all. Because my computer wasn't very good, I made a deal with a student. If she would let me have unrestricted use of her computer—a much better machine—I would help her with her final papers. She agreed, and the woman I was dating at the time also cleared her schedule as much as she could (she was also a student) to help me edit the manuscript. I'd drive to use the computer, make changes, and print out the pages. Then I'd head back to my apartment to read it over. If there were mistakes, I'd get back in my car and drive back to the student's place to input the changes, print it again, and read it. This process would go on until, sometimes, one or two in the morning, when the student would finally tell me I had to get the hell out so that she could go to sleep. I'd laugh and head home knowing I'd start the process over again the next day. I didn't see very many people during this process. I didn't have time to socialize.

After long days and nights of reading, typing, and editing with the help of a couple of good friends, I turned in the project and was done. Kaufman read the dissertation and approved the revisions. I took a copy to David Hall and waited for him to send his approval. Appiah was more difficult to track down, but I became a regular visitor to his office until he read the revisions and gave his approval. I had the signed forms, got the dissertation copied in accordance with school regulations, and took the copies to the registrar's office. I was tired, but I was also done!

I still had some time before commencement when I'd get the degree and be known as "Dr. Anthony Bernard Pinn"—just "Dr.," no "Reverend" in front of it. On the day of commencement, dressed in my crimson robe and feeling pretty good, I ran across Gordon Kaufman and his wife headed to the Divinity School. They stopped and hugged me. He left to get ready for the procession of faculty. She, however, lagged behind and told me that she knew he'd been hard on me, but that I should understand he did it because he was ready to retire and wanted to help me through the program before he left, or I might not make it through. His students were vulnerable, she told me. His opponents left on campus after his retirement might take their disagreement with him out on his students, including me.

Image 11. The author and his mother after PhD commencement ceremony.

Neither Kaufman nor his wife, Dorothy, could know how much I appreciated her words and his actions. I determined at that point whatever I ended up doing, I would have the same commitment to those under my guidance. I'd look out for them as he had looked out for me, but I might make it a bit more transparent—as best I could—than he had.

In all, I developed a way of thinking and acting that was consistent with my convictions expressed through solid academic work. It was a freedom to think and act that had been unavailable—or of no interest—to the ministers I was leaving behind. Even Baptist ministers who worked in organizations that were all about local autonomy could be kicked out of the church for the wrong action or statement. Perhaps this is why so many in ministry played it safe and when pushed on issues during private conversations or in the classroom would respond, feigning frustration, "The people aren't ready . . ." This statement is made as if they, the clergy, are ready, and they are simply awaiting the mysterious movement of the congregation to a similar spiritual and intellectual state. They pretend to be spiritually advanced but held back by the limits of their people to appreciate and work with a greater vision of Christian faith and action. In this case, a fake sense of spiritual superiority is the best defense against hard work and questions to their authority.

To me, ministers seemed unwilling and not ready to challenge the people in their churches or to answer the questions congregants were actually asking because rigorous challenges might lead to people leaving for churches where it was all praise and no thinking. The monetary health of their churches (and their private compensation) would suffer. It was better to keep congregants pacified than have them run the risk of revolt.

Many ministers, I suspect, feared that their pastoral challenge to the congregation would be met with the force of an equal challenge from the people. Something like "Push us to be better and do more, and we'll push you to lead us so that we can meet the challenge. More work from us means more work from you!" I'd come to recognize that creative answers to contemporary problems beyond "letting the people get happy" during the sermon requires ministers to be more than weekend warriors. They might have to rethink and, perhaps, double, their commitment to making a concrete, physical difference in their communities beyond the walls of the church. I'd been in the church long enough to know that pastors might whine and complain about the hard work and "unreasonable" demands placed on them by a thinking congregation. But who cares? Do the job or find a new one.

The death of the symbol God left a lot of space to fill and new responsibilities for the nurturing of life. I was trying to figure all this out as I shifted from a career in the church to a career in the academy as a professor of religion . . . who didn't believe in the gods and traditions about which he would lecture and write.

Chapter Thirteen

MINNESOTA . . . NOT SO NICE

It was 1993, and I was so nervous about the job market. If I didn't get a job, what would I do? In the back of my mind was the fear that the church people I'd left behind would see my unemployment (if I didn't get a job) as a sign of God's existence and greatness—and the stupidity of my decision to leave the church. There would be sermons celebrating my hardship as a sign of God's goodness.

I combed the American Academy of Religion job listings. That organization was *the* place for job postings in my area of study. Whenever I saw something even remotely related, I started working on an application. I would write draft after draft of my application letter, doing my best to point out how and why I was the perfect person for the job. I tailored my curriculum vitae to highlight my educational pedigree, fellowships won, lectures given, and my teaching experience. I toiled over my writing samples. The documents had to capture their attention without giving away too many of my ideas; I feared someone might take one of my ideas and run with it.

I assumed my professors would write outstanding letters of recommendation. In fact, when requesting letters I explicitly asked if they would be able to write me an "excellent" letter. I couldn't leave anything to chance.

I wasn't alone in applying for jobs, and I'd have to have casual, if somewhat awkward, conversations with other students. The campus was small enough to make it impossible to avoid other people who were interested in the same jobs. So we'd make guarded comments, not wanting to seem too interested, trying to play it easy. The civility masked a strong survival instinct. "Yeah, that job might be a good start, but I've heard some bad things about that department" or "I'm considering applying." These types of comments were meant to throw people off, to avoid showing too much excitement in case the job went to someone else. Guarded comments left me with some wiggle room, a way to ward off disappointment if I didn't get that job. But I *really* wanted a job and I got some relief when I was invited for a campus interview at Macalester College in Saint Paul, Minnesota. I went, gave my lecture, led a class, and talked with faculty and students—all in an effort to convince them that I was the person for the job.

On December 24, I received a phone call at my mother's house. It was the provost at Macalester offering me a job. I let other schools know that I had a job offer, and this gave them a few options: tell me they weren't that far along and take me off the list or move things along and bring me to campus as quickly as possible. The second option was the one taken by Bowdoin College.

I decided to accept the Macalester offer. I would have better compensation than at Bowdoin, freedom to teach what I wanted to teach, and the school was located in a city. The job wasn't in religious history as advertised, however. That one went to someone else, but David Hopper, a theologian in the Religious Studies Department at Macalester, began the process of retirement, which freed up a tenure-track line they used to hire me.

After commencement, I packed up my things, loaded them in my Nissan Pulsar, and said good-bye to my friends. Some of them, like Benjamin Valentin, who I met at the Divinity School, and Eli Valentin I'd see regularly over the years, and they became more like brothers than just friends. I'm connected in a deep and abiding way to them and their wives, Karina and Maria. Ben and I have worked on a good number of projects together, and Eli and I hang out whenever I make it to New York City. Ben and Eli were born there, and I adopted it as my second home.

On my way to Saint Paul, I drove from Boston to Buffalo to see my mother. Her health was declining, so I tried to get home as often as I could. She was proud of me for finishing school and proud that I had a job that paid me more than she'd ever made. For her, this was progress, a sign that she'd done things right—despite me leaving the church and not believing in God. After some time with her, I continued the drive, staying for a day in Wisconsin before arriving on the Macalester campus.

I had a job, a place to call home, and an office. I was proud of all three. The office was the first I'd ever had. There was a department secretary who handled some of the responsibilities I'd always done for myself. And I'd walk from my house just a couple of minutes away and think to myself, "Well, you're a professor now, a professional thinker. Damn!" I had a good set of colleagues in the small Religious Studies Department, but also in History, English, Political Science, and the "hard" sciences. The campus was small, and we talked across disciplinary lines; it was the only way to get work done and to remain true to the interdisciplinary nature of a liberal arts education, as Macalester understood it.

I wanted my students to experience me as informed, smart, and engaging. And I had to fight the occasional assumption that I didn't have the training my colleagues had or the occasional student who wanted to pretend that I was his "colleague" and that we were somehow equals. The fact that Macalester had a first-name culture didn't help with any of this. Early on I tried to get around this culture of familiarity when I told students that they should address me the way they addressed . . . I tried to come up with the most senior member of the faculty I could think of as the example. I remembered the chair of my department and my friend, Calvin Roetzel, and asked "How do you address him?" One of the students looked at me and said, "You mean Cal?" The others nodded in agreement, and I knew it was over. The campus culture would win, and I'd have to find other ways of staking my claim.

On a campus like Macalester, there was a delicate balance between being a tough authority figure and being approachable. Getting this balance right was important because student opinions mattered. So much about our teaching evaluations involved the students and popularity: do the students like you? And who knew what would turn the tables from like to dislike? Tied to this was avoiding misplaced attraction on the part of students in a campus culture that involved close contact and sponsored meetings in faculty homes. I managed all of this as best I could: fitting into campus culture while protecting myself from anything that could threaten my job.

While Macalester was a liberal environment, issues of race and class still played out, and it was important for me to negotiate these situations well—whether with other faculty, administrators, or students. I couldn't come off as the irrational, angry black man who couldn't be dealt with, but I also wouldn't let people get away with stupidity. I had to deal with political issues on campus, mindful that I was new, without tenure, and vulnerable. Minnesota had a reputation for being "nice," but this wasn't necessarily a posture with any depth. It was superficial, as far as I could tell.

For instance, my house was located on the edge of campus in an area known as "Tangle town," a haphazard layout of streets. It was solidly middle class and overwhelmingly white. My first few days, I wanted to get familiar with my new city, and so I'd walk around the neighborhood. More than once, one of my neighbors came outside and asked me if I was lost and if they could help me get somewhere. My initial thought was "How helpful, how nice," until I thought about it after each encounter: under the smile and the offer of assistance was a more vicious statement: "You clearly don't belong here, so let me help you leave." It annoyed me, but the "Why are you here" was said in such a nice way that to respond with annoyance or anger would have made me seem like the bad guy.

The problem wasn't limited to my immediate surroundings. My first trip to the Mall of America, that giant collection of shops and restaurants on the edge of the city, involved a run-in with security. It's an intimidating place and hard to maneuver, so I was at a kiosk looking at the map of shops when two mall security guards approached me. Mind you, I wasn't the only person confused and looking at the map, but they directed their attention to me and asked, "Can we help you find something?" Again, my initial thought was, "Damn, these Minnesotans are considerate." After responding that I didn't need help and continuing to move around the mall, it hit me: they had singled me out, the black guy at the kiosk. Another possible interpretation of the question: "You should know we are watching you."

I'd encountered race-based questions and comments in New York and certainly in Boston, but there was a difference in Minneapolis–St. Paul. In the other cities the comments could be challenged as openly as they were made, but in Minnesota the pretense of humor ("I'm kidding!") or the pretext of concern ("Can I help you out of here?") restricted response to annoyance pushed below the surface.

Getting used to these kinds of encounters wasn't easy, but I knew I needed to develop a way of keeping those comments and attitudes from ripping me apart, from eating away at me. I addressed my predicament by talking with an inner circle of friends. They let me get it out of my system—complain about the passive-aggressive approach to conflict in Minneapolis–St. Paul, complain about the cold weather, the short summers, and the endless supply of mosquitoes during the warm weather. Those conversations alone weren't enough, so I also tried as best I could to keep my home a space away from campus. This was hard in a culture of faculty opening their homes to students, and it was particularly difficult for me because I was single and living just a couple of minutes from my office.

From my college-owned house, I could hear the bagpipes playing in preparation for games and special events; I could hear the football games, and I could hear and see the students walking back and forth between classes. I never felt like I really left campus. But I tried to the best of my abilities to keep something about my home and my personal life private in a place where everyone felt entitled to know whatever they wanted to know about you. And if you didn't share information, they were the wronged party, and you were the inconsiderate and offensive one.

Despite all this, there were things to enjoy about my campus life. I looked forward to being in my office, with the sun coming through the window (even during the heart of winter), with music playing as I sat at the computer, writing. Although there was an open-door policy meant to encourage students to stop by and talk with faculty, I kept my door closed as much as possible to avoid the "Hey, I have a few minutes before class, so let's talk" interruptions. Weekends on campus were better because there were few people around; I could turn the music up and work without interruption. I learned from Calvin Roetzel to take advantage of the quiet time to get the articles and books written that would not only secure my future at Macalester but that would also get me recognized beyond the campus. It was a beautiful campus, and I had good colleagues and a supportive administration. There were plenty of events on campus to keep us entertained and informed, and I enjoyed attending them when I could.

Some said I spent too much time working, or that I was writing too quickly and that could be a problem. By *quickly* they meant thin and nonsubstantive work. But as far as I was concerned, they were wrong. Ever since my time as a graduate student I had a particular relationship with writing: I had to get words on the page. I would write until everything I thought or wondered about a subject was down on paper. I didn't feel comfortable or relaxed, had a hard time thinking about other things, until I'd purged my mind of those ideas and committed them to a first draft. For me, this was a good life, and it centered comfortably on my computer and my books. Writing wasn't a chore; I loved it.

Don't get me wrong; I wasn't a hermit. Other things mattered to me, but everything was measured against my life as an academic. I was a bit cold-blooded on this score: people could come and go, but my commitment to my professional life was always in the forefront. Nothing, and no one, could be allowed to jeopardize it.

For the most part, I had the life I believed I wanted. And to the extent office and home could be spaces I could keep to myself, they were the places in my life I favored.

On campus, even with the need to be leery of politics, there was a bit of breathing room and an opportunity to refine my thinking on humanism and my relationship to it. I was free to teach whatever I wanted to teach, and so my courses revolved around different aspects of African American religion as well as religion and popular culture. My classes were a good size based on the school's enrollment, but they weren't so large that I had a difficult time managing them. The department was supportive, and administrators were concerned with my development. But in order to secure my job, I had to take my love for writing and my dissertation, and combine them into a published book. Macalester College is a liberal arts institution where teaching is important, but it has its version of the "publish or perish" structure. I had to get my dissertation published, and I had five years to do it in order to receive tenure and a job for life.

I didn't have a lot of information about the process of turning my dissertation into a book, but I met an editor from Continuum Publishing Group (now an imprint of Bloomsbury) during one of the conferences I attended as a graduate student. After a conversation about my post-graduation plans, she asked me to send her a copy of my dissertation once it was approved. Delighted to have someone interested in reading it, I agreed to send it during the summer.

After commencement and after putting a copy of my dissertation in the mail, I forgot all about it and focused my energy into preparing for Macalester. While I was settling in to my new life in Minnesota, the department secretary gave me a message that had come through her voice mail. It was from the editor at Continuum offering me a contract for my dissertation. Shortly after receiving the contract, I signed it and sent it back. I spent a little time working on revisions, listening to blues music for inspiration to get the right tone. These were minor changes, and within a short period, the manuscript was off to the press.

I wondered what would become of the published book. I hoped it would make some sort of splash and that it would generate conversation and perhaps increase sensitivity to humanism as an important part of African American life and thought. I knew philosopher William R. Jones's book had met with opposition from some and was dismissed by others. And he had stopped attending two of the most important professional gatherings for people involved in the study of religion and the study of African American religion. I don't know for certain if he stopped attending because of the negative reaction to his work, but it seems a plausible possibility. If the reaction to my work was the same, however, I was determined to remain involved, to not be pushed to the sidelines by those representing the dominant perspective on African American religion as always theistic and centered on the black church. I'd be tough and stand my ground.

A published book meant the potential of a much larger audience, and once it was out there, I couldn't control the ideas and couldn't determine what people did with them. That thought was both stressful and exciting. It would be my first book, my first humanist statement as a professional.

When the book came out, I sent copies to friends and my family. My mother was so happy she asked her friends to get copies. I sent a copy to the Lucas family, and they were proud, but nothing about their response ever suggested they'd actually read it. In general, the reaction from the church people I'd grown up knowing made it clear they didn't read the book; they were just proud that someone they knew had written a book.

Still, I was denouncing the religious and theological precepts they held dear, and I knew these people well enough to know that such challenges were met with denouncements and threats of hellfire. I received none of this from them, just smiles and words of congratulations for this great accomplishment.

The response from my colleagues in the study of African American religion was more mixed. Some said kind things about the strengths of the book. Others accused me of a range of things from "intellectual masturbation" to selling out and losing sight of what it means to be black. Mind you, these weren't comments made in private conversations over coffee. They were public remarks at professional meetings, and they were meant—one could assume—to put me in my place and to maintain the dominance of the "party line."

If they got loud, I got louder. I gave papers at the major meetings supporting my point, each time trying to refine my argument. I pushed for humanism, but I needed to be clearer in what I meant by humanism and how people made use of it in their lives.

When making my revisions to the manuscript, I'd come across a couple of humanist and atheist groups, and I'd reached out to them but had gotten no response expressing much interest in my work. A guy studying religion and writing a first book on humanism wasn't as important to them as, say, the contributions of high-profile scientists who were fighting superstition and supernaturalism. And, on top of this, there seemed to be little agreement regarding what humanism is and what it means.

Some groups argued it's a secular perspective akin to atheism, and for others humanism didn't by definition rule out some elements of theism—like belief in some type of supreme power. I jumped into the debate arguing that humanism, for African Americans, replaced traditional forms of religion. In this argument was my suggestion that humanism could serve as an alternate form of religion, providing African Americans with everything religion provided but without any of its major difficulties and shortcomings. Humanism provided everything necessary for a productive life. It had an ethical center, moral codes, ritual structures, a history, and traditions.

At this early stage I borrowed the idea that the "human is the measure of all things" as a fundamental way of thinking about humanism. But I said this with a sense of realism, noting that humans are guilty of great harm such as racism, sexism, homophobia, and so on. And this recognition means that we have to show humility regarding what humanity might achieve and the limits of its reach. The human is the measure of all things simply because we are only able to encounter the world and work within the world, to relate to the world, as humans. We can't step outside of our humanity to view and address the world. That's all I meant by the statement.

I wasn't certain how many minds I changed with my work, and I hadn't given any thought to media attention for my ideas. It wasn't anything I'd been trained to deal with, and it wasn't something that faculty talked about or, as far as I could tell, sought out at Macalester. I was thoughtful and as coopera- tive as I could be when reporters called or e-mailed for a quick comment on some church development or for perspective on some local or national reli- gious issue or crisis that was hot at the moment.

So I was surprised when I received a call from the Minneapolis *StarTribune* wanting more than just a quick statement. The reporter said she'd heard about me and wanted to do a profile piece for a Saturday issue of the paper. She wanted to write a profile piece . . . on me? Why me?

I was a little nervous, but more curious, and of course who wouldn't be at least a little excited by the attention. So I agreed. We set a day and time when I wasn't teaching. Dressed in jeans and a sweater, I opened the door and invited her into my office.

The interview was fairly long and began like you would expect: questions about my home, my family, my education, and my friends. We transitioned to questions about my teaching: what courses do I teach? Why do I teach African American religion? Is there something unique about African American reli- gion? How do I like teaching at Macalester? What is the response of students to my classes? I went through the list, saying a bit about the courses I offer and why I offer them. I gave the politically correct responses concerning life in Minneapolis–St. Paul and at Macalester in particular: "It's an interesting time in my life, and I'm looking forward to learning more about the Twin Cities and about Macalester."

Then she turned attention to my research. We talked about my disserta- tion and my first book. I outlined the history of African American humanism and the subject's merit for wrestling with theological issues and ways to promote justice and social transformation. She asked about reception of the book within the academy and in the public, and I told her about some of the written reviews and conference discussions, but without much detail. Her readers didn't need that much information. They needed enough to give them a sense of the book and hopefully to spark an interest in reading it. She asked me about future projects. I had a few in mind and a couple in the works, so I said something about them, trying to avoid jargon and make the projects sound interesting for the readers.

Then there was a pause before she asked me about my personal beliefs. I think she assumed I was a Christian: Here's a guy who teaches religion, and although he studies humanism, he must believe in God, right? Why would someone teach and study religion if he isn't religious? Some people have a difficult time distinguishing between church school and the college classroom. And everyone has an opinion on religion and feels free to share it as if their personal attendance of some religious organization is comparable to my years of training. People go to religious services because they are religious; wouldn't someone teach religion because they are religious? Yet how many assume the person teaching Marxism is a Marxist?

Her question was straightforward. And it went something like this: "Dr. Pinn, are you a religious person? Are you a Christian?"

I wanted to be careful but honest. "No, I'm not a Christian." This was my opening.

I told the reporter that I teach religion and give a lot of classroom time and research to different theistic traditions within African American communities. And I do so because they have had and continue to have cultural value. Theism in its various forms has had an undeniable influence on and importance to African Americans, and this role should generate critical attention to the nature and meaning of these traditions. So I study them. However, I told her, I don't personally agree with them, and I don't believe they are theologically and doctrinally accurate. I think these traditions tend to do more harm than good. I told her this hadn't always been my position, that I'd been a preacher who started in the pulpit when I was about twelve and remained in the church for a good number of years. I preached, prayed, and taught the Bible and its codes for as long as I could, and then I left because what the church—and theism in general—offered me didn't amount to much.

Now I am a humanist, or what some would call an atheist. (At that time, I didn't make a clear distinction between the two.) She listened without interruption, but I could tell she was at least a little thrown by my shift from being a good preacher to being a committed humanist.

We ended the conversation, and, before leaving, she told me the photographer would call to make arrangements to take some pictures they'd use with the story. The pictures were taken, the story written, and I waited for it to be published.

I didn't think it would mean much to anyone beyond my immediate family and small circle of friends—maybe a few of my colleagues on campus. Who'd be interested in the story of this professor at a small liberal arts college who teaches and doesn't personally believe the truth of the traditions he teaches? And the story was to appear on Saturday—a slow news day. Wouldn't people have better things to do than read about me?

The day the interview was published, I was driving along with a couple of my friends, one I'd known since Boston days, and the other, Richard Ammons, had recently joined Macalester as Vice President for College Advancement. We were fraternity brothers of Alpha Phi Alpha (I'd pledged while at Harvard), headed to brunch. I sat in the front with Richard driving and read the story to them. We thought nothing of it—a nice story, but nothing memorable.

On Monday, some of my voice mails suggested that some people found troubling my thinking about religion. The gloves were off; Minnesota nice was done, and people were ready to speak their minds. Some condemned me to hell straightaway, while others tried to convince me to rethink my position so as to avoid hell. Within a few days, the hate mail began to arrive. It was more of the same: repent or hell, and so on. Letters condemning me for my godless life and raising questions concerning the morality of letting an atheist teach religion. Calls for my firing or at least punishment were a common rejoinder to the article.

There were no more invitations to have "hot dish." Some Minnesotans lost their niceness over this issue. The president of the college, Michael McPherson, however, called to let me know that he supported me and would always honor academic freedom. He wanted me to feel confident that I was in no jeopardy because of the story. Calvin Roetzel also expressed his support for me and reiterated the president's assurance that this would have no negative consequences for me, even though it was taking place around the time of my review.

At least one colleague wasn't so generous. He had the nerve to reprimand me for the story and my opinion, and how it embarrassed him at his church. He wanted to know why I didn't ask the religious studies department for permission to talk to the reporter. Permission? Trying to remain calm, I reminded him that I wasn't his child but a grown man. I was his colleague, not his ward, and I didn't need anyone's permission to speak my mind. I would say what I wanted, when I wanted, and how I wanted.

The college chaplain was far from happy as well; I found out that I had been the subject of several Sunday sermons. I imagine some ministers condemned me, and others encouraged prayer for my soul.

Some students were upset, not because of my personal perspective on theism but because their parents weren't comfortable with them taking instruction from an atheist.

Not all the Minnesotans hated me as a result of my humanist stance. In fact, I met my now ex-wife because of the article. She called to see if she could buy me a soda. We were together for some years after that . . . until we weren't.

There were a few calls asking me to appear on television; one was for a kind of "gotcha" national television program, which I declined. A few of the atheist and humanist organizations with which I'd tried to make contact earlier reached out to me to congratulate me on the story and to express their interest in being in communication. I'd "earned" their notice, but it would be a good number of years before I would become involved with them in any significant way. At this point, I was glad for the contact but disappointed that it took this stressful situation to get their notice.

There were also humanists and atheists in the Twin Cities who shared my struggle and perspective and wanted to celebrate what they understood as my courage and forthrightness. They were interested in hearing more of my story. I imagine they hadn't encountered very many African American humanists, and they were curious as to what unbelief meant for African Americans, and how they, white Minnesotans, might connect with the like-minded from marginalized race groups. I received and accepted invitations to speak to their groups.

At some of these meetings, I had to field what I would call ignorant questions and assumptions regarding African Americans, one of the most offensive being the ridiculous argument that humanism and atheism were highly intellectual positions and African Americans were too emotional to appreciate and embrace either one. African Americans, some attendees said with confidence to a well-educated African American, crave the energy and rituals of the church. This came too close to the "Sing a spiritual for us, Uncle Jim," attitude toward African Americans as objects for entertainment—childlike and highly emotional. I had expected better, but the confidence with which these statements were made, the speakers looking directly in the face of an African American, was staggering. These were for the most part well-read, informed, and educated people, but they were still saddled with backward notions concerning racial differences. I felt sad and embarrassed for those making these claims because they were so delusional· and uninformed. Yet there was no good excuse for their willful ignorance, so I was also angry with them—these people who, despite considering themselves highly intellectual and dedicated to information gathering, were content with eighteenth-century ideas on race, intelligence, and civilization.

Although their understanding was flawed and lacked the depth of what I brought to the humanist table, those who reached out to me did point to the possibility of community, of relationships based on shared values. For the first time, my sense of humanist connections extended well beyond a few figures here and there or historical developments at a distance from my circumstances. It wasn't an easy fit. I wasn't as open to the possibility of divinity as some humanists, but I wasn't an atheist easily placed in the "New Atheism" camp either.

As I understood it, New Atheism atheists denounced religion in a sweeping fashion and tended to be more aggressive in promoting their critiques. Any talk of ritual was met with quick resistance because they weren't religious and rituals had everything to do with religion. They were against God and in favor of science, rejected any special status for religious organizations, and wanted to keep religion out of the public area/public policy. So many humanists held to a separation of church and state agenda, although they were also worried that commitment to science could easily turn into scientism. I believed rejection of superstition and supernatural claims wasn't the end of the conversation but was only the beginning, a starting point that had to be followed quickly with attention to what humanists and atheists believe, and what those human values *do* in the world.

And while some humanists/atheists like me left theistic organizations because of their antihuman theology and supernaturalism, we continued to believe cooperation and collaboration on a shared concern with the integrity of life could bring theists and nontheists together to work on important community projects. This didn't amount to a permanent, or even stable, connection but rather temporary practices of solidarity during which philosophical and theological disagreements remain but are bracketed for the sake of a larger agenda. This seemed to me a mature way to handle both the disagreements between theists and humanists/atheists as well as our shared need to preserve the integrity of life.

Humanists were mocked at times for being too soft on religion and too accommodating to theists; atheists were critiqued for being too single-minded with respect to religion and too lacking in concern for sociopolitical issues beyond the dominance of science and the need for religion to die away from both the public arena and private life. I can't say that I didn't participate in these debates, but I can say they didn't matter that much to me. Growing a useful framing of humanism by getting my ideas out wasn't dependent on who won the debate. Both sides were missing something.

I didn't believe that humanists and theists couldn't ever disagree; I simply thought their disputes should be productive with some agreed-upon ground rules. If nothing else, that type of constructive debate might help both camps better define themselves and—I would hope—recognize the overlap in their agendas. That overlap would then constitute the common vision for collaborative thinking and working. This sounded like a good idea, at least to an academic who often worked in abstractions.

My goals for solidarity weren't based on years in the trenches of secular activism in the Midwest. My objectives were somewhat idyllic and a bit marginal. I had the right pedigree and I offered them a way into diversity, to the extent they could claim me as one of their own, but this only meant so much in terms of my ability to redirect the conversation.

The media attention and fallout from my interview also brought me into contact with more of the Macalester community. Two people in particular—Ramon Rentas and Robbie Seals—became steadfast friends, and Ramon in particular has remained a valuable conversation partner (more like a brother). He doesn't hold to my perspective on God, but he pushes and critiques—and he had kind things to say when too many Minnesotans made venomous attacks on my character and place in the profession. There wasn't enough "hot dish" or lutefisk to make up for this nastier side of life in the Twin Cities.

Figuring out how to fit within humanist/atheist communities was only part of my new battle. There were African Americans for whom my lack of belief in God placed me outside the black community. To them, I'd surrendered the African American tradition and had embraced a Eurocentric view of the world. By this they meant "black folk" aren't and have never been atheists and humanists. Those two categories are impositions and problematic implementations of "white ways" of being and thinking. African Americans survived (and thrive) because of theism, they were quick to report, and it is through theism—particularly in the form of the black church—that the identity of African Americans is most vividly portrayed and protected. To leave the black church is to surrender one's identity as a member of *the* African American community with all the rights and privileges therein. African Americans who embraced Islam in some way, African-based traditions, Judaism, or any number of theistic orientations weren't as favored as Christians, but they got a "pass" on the issue of belonging. They were close enough and still recognizable as people of "faith." But the atheists and the humanists occupied a different geography altogether. I clearly didn't agree, but I understood their perspective in that it was something I'd held to years ago, when I was in the church.

While this is bad enough, the assumption that humanists and atheists like me should be apologetic about our take on life is insult added to injury, but again, it is something I would have expected from atheists and humanists when I was an evangelical Christian.

People like me, atheists and humanists, are to appreciate the traditions of theists, sit quietly in their church services, and smile as activity after activity takes place contrary to everything we embrace as proper and healthy ways of thinking. We are expected to accept it when our commitments are disrespected, but the congeniality isn't returned. Theists are free to mock and dismiss humanism and atheism. It is as if losing belief in God and all its trappings removes our humanity and frees others from obligation to respect us.

Some might argue that I am overstating the case, but I don't think so, not in light of the way I experienced both sides of the issue. There's too much in the public record, let alone anecdotal information, to support the way a theism norm shapes perceptions of what it means to be black and how those who don't fit can be treated. In a small number of cases, I was charged with allowing Western ideas gathered through my education to warp my thinking and take away my blackness. Reading books about whites and by whites, written from a "white" perspective had made whiteness normative for me and, critics implied, I now wanted to be white.

All of this is ridiculous! As if being a humanist or atheist means surrendering one's membership card into black communities. Of course this is nonsense, but it is a widespread assumption, and I had to address it for personal and professional reasons. I still have my card, but I just came to recognize that there are so many ways to express one's blackness—and blackness doesn't require church.

I wasn't departing a particular community but rather was showing the long-standing diversity of that community. I was celebrating that diversity, respecting difference as a positive, theism and nontheism. There is, and has been for as long as there have been African Americans, something that can be understood as African American humanism and African American atheism. And I was determined to say as much as possible about both.

Chapter Fourteen

ENTER THE UUA

Before my interview with the Minneapolis *StarTribune* was published, I knew little about the Unitarian Universalist Association (UUA), only what I'd gathered from the UU students on the Harvard Divinity School campus.

Although I assumed there had to be some sort of theological glue holding the UUA religious world together, I was thrown by what appeared to me to be so much theological flexibility within its structure. The UUA prides itself on its philosophy of deeds being more important than particular creeds and doctrines, and so people with a variety of beliefs—including atheism—are encouraged to participate. I knew nothing about its Sunday worship services, and my effort to embrace my emerging humanism didn't involve a great interest in experimenting with another church—even a church that considered itself fully open to all patterns of belief. But after the nastiness I'd encountered once my humanist stance had been made public, the kindness coming from the UUA was welcomed.

While some UUA folks just wanted me to know they were sending good wishes and would welcome an opportunity to talk a bit more over a cup of coffee, others invited me to come to their service and talk to the congregation about my views on humanism. By accepting these invitations, I wouldn't be preaching, as I'd done with other engagements in the past; these would be more like the lectures I gave on a regular basis on and off campus. The only difference would be the day, Sunday morning, and the venue, a church. I started with First Unitarian Society, a major force in the larger association.

I wasn't certain what to expect, but I was happy for the opportunity to tell my story.

The Sunday of my talk, I was introduced to the congregation. It wasn't a "black church" type of introduction. Those tend to be almost as dramatic and as preachy as the actual sermon. This featured the measured tones and intellectual profile that mark the introduction of speakers at conferences and other academic events.

I was welcomed with applause, and I moved toward the lectern—no kneeling to pray beforehand. I could tell my story without the aid of notes. I'd learned to preach with an outline and was more than comfortable with that; I lectured in the classroom based on that model. This was more personal; no outline required.

I moved through the story of my early years in the church, and the audience seemed particularly responsive to the idea of a preteen preacher. It wasn't that they got loud, or said "Amen," or responded in any of the other ways so familiar to me during my church days. The looks on their faces, the way they leaned forward in their chairs and so on gave me a sense of what they were thinking: "A child preacher?" I knew what they must have been asking themselves at that point: "What can a kid possibly say in a ministerial context that is meaningful? How can someone that young have a handle on theology in a way that would equip him to preach?" Telling them that I was ordained in college only added to the surprise. I didn't know anything about their ordination process when I addressed them that Sunday, but I would come to learn it was nothing an eighteen-year-old could have undertaken and completed. I described the frustration and growing discomfort as my evangelical theology and practices began to fall short, and this was met with nods of agreement and solidarity. As I finished my presentation and moved away from the lectern, people stood and clapped. I was thankful and grateful for the encouragement.

At another local Unitarian Universalist church, I encountered an order of service similar to the churches I knew as a child, with songs, moments of meditation, greeting people, and the "talk," but without any real mention of divine forces and personal salvation.

Telling my story wasn't the same as preaching, but it was therapeutic and affirming. It allowed me to pull together the strands of my life in a private/

public way. These invitations and corresponding talks also got me thinking about Unitarian Universalism. Most of the people associated with it seemed nice enough, encouraging and supportive, and with each encounter there was an invitation to join them.

They would say in passing that I wouldn't have the same "problems" with their association that I'd experienced in the past with my AME churches. There would be no push for the theism I'd rejected; they were open to various truths and committed to social action and justice work. They'd say with a smile, "After all, our motto is deeds, not creeds." While that was true, looking out at the congregation and being mindful of the people trying to "recruit" me, I felt like something was missing. I didn't see very many people who looked like me, and I heard some ignorant comments about African American religiosity and emotional bent—from just a few, but they were memorable all the same.

I might not have the theism problem with the UUA, but would there be cultural dissonance and social misunderstandings? Would I be alone racially and, because of that, somewhat marginalized? Would I be exchanging one bag of problems for another, just when I'd finally gotten detangled from church-related drama? These questions where big for me, and I wasn't eager to dive into the UUA. But I didn't dismiss the possibility either. I'd think about it—no rush, but I'd consider it.

I met Koren Arisian at First Unitarian Society. He was the former minister and a thoughtful and reflective man. We'd meet periodically for lunch, just to talk. He also thought the UUA would be a good home for me—a win-win for me and for the association. He didn't push, but he did take time to point out the benefits and virtues of the association and its theology. Koren acknowledged what I had come to know through a little research of my own, that the UUA hadn't done such a great job on issues of race earlier in the twentieth century. However, he quickly continued, it had made strides to correct for this and had invested time and money into doing better work on appreciating and expanding its racial diversity. He'd always conclude with a smile and say, no organization is perfect, but this one is open to improvement.

One of my former professors at Harvard Divinity School, Sharon Welch, was a member of the UUA, and she also supported the idea that it might be of real benefit to me. She was responsible for some of my academic development and opinions, and I knew we had similar theological and ethical ideas, all of which meant I had to take seriously what she said about the association's potential to be a good fit for me. But the diversity issue still bothered me.

I listened to them both, as well as a bunch of others, asked a good number of questions, and attended the occasional service. I'd spent many years in the church, and my struggle with church involvement was still fresh for me, so I needed to be certain. I wouldn't go through a bad church experience again. After all, it was clear to me I could live and live well without that type of community.

I continued this flirtation with the UUA until I reached an odd point in my life some years later when I felt a deep desire to join. As inexplicable as it was to me, I went with it. I was visiting faculty at Rice University, living between Minneapolis and Houston, and I felt a strong need for ritual and community. Perhaps I felt alone in a new context and wanted some stability? I'm not certain why I had this feeling, this desire to connect, but I did. And so, after attending several services, I filled out the form, arranging a meeting with one of the ministers in charge. We met; I signed the book and pledged financial support. I was a member.

There were differences between UU congregations, with some being theistic (basically Christian) and others being aggressively humanistic, if not atheistic in orientation. The church I'd joined was the latter, but the Sunday services, worship services in general, didn't vary in a significant way from the theistic black church services of my past. Sure, there was no shouting, no dancing in the spirit, and no energetic sermons about God or God's involvement in the world. There was no reliance on the Bible as a special book that had the answers to all our questions. The songs we sang didn't mention God; they were about humans and life in general. Hymns celebrated human creativity and ingenuity and placed human animals within the context of the larger web of life. We didn't have Communion to celebrate the death of Jesus the Christ, nor did we have prayer at the altar. Instead, we had moments of sharing and meditation. It wasn't simply that songs were sung or that there was a time of meditation and sharing. The similarities were more substantive than that. Time was marked out in a similar fashion, and the tone of the gathering felt familiar—reminiscent of my old church experience. The theological language was different in that it didn't have the same strong Christian vocabulary, and that was because of the UUA embrace of many different "spiritual" orientations—but religious grammar still guided that ritual space in a way that seemed to push attention beyond the mere bodies occupying the seats.

The ministers proceeded into the sanctuary each Sunday, and if your eyes followed them to the pulpit, you wouldn't encounter any of the traditional signs of the church. There were no crosses, no stained glass windows depicting biblical stories, and there were no images of saints and the like. Their robes were similar to those worn by other ministers in other denominations. They sat in seats in the pulpit in the larger churches that looked familiar to me, similar to those I knew growing up in the church in Buffalo and then New York and Boston.

I'd left the Christian Church but by going to UU services, it wasn't clear that I'd actually gone very far away. These services were lighter versions of what I'd experienced. The basic structures were the same; they were simply named differently. This humanist church didn't take me far enough away from the Sunday mornings I'd experienced as a theist. There wasn't enough that spoke to the naturalist aspect of ritual and thought; there wasn't enough for me that pointed to a rugged humanism. For others, I'm sure, the nature of Sunday morning in this particular church fit the bill, but it didn't give me the experience I wanted. When this was combined with what I saw as an awkward approach to issues of diversity marking the UUA, I was left wanting.

I wanted my humanism, my atheism, to mean a different way of forging community, and a different way of relating to the world. With a radically different theology and a sense of ethics above static doctrine, why didn't the UUA have a more distinct approach to ritual gatherings and community?

Shouldn't there be a link between the claim of ethics as privileged and the look as well as the content of time spent together on a Sunday? Here's a thought, a centering of "deeds over creeds" might even mean the end of formal Sunday gatherings because each day is an opportunity to live out this UUA approach of deeds as being favored over creeds. By doing so, there would be no need to single out Sunday as special. Let the theists have it as a special day during which, at least for a few hours, they can deny that they have bodies that matter, and they can concentrate on the souls imprisoned in those bodies. Our Sundays, as humanists and atheists, don't need to mark out special time the way it must for theists.

I was a member of a congregation, and I tried to attend somewhat regularly, but I found myself almost dreading services. The activities—particularly the Sunday worship—couldn't compete with an opportunity for a run on a bright, sunny morning, or a leisurely breakfast with friends, or an opportunity to catch up on the television programming I enjoyed, like *CBS Sunday Morning*. These other activities reinforced the embodied nature of life within the world; they spoke to a sense of time and space that was ordinary but rich with meaning for me. I felt the weight of my body and my body in connection with the world in a much stronger way through these activities. Church didn't provide me with a similar encounter with the world that left the mundane, mundane, and the ordinary, ordinary. I maintain a relationship with the UUA even though I stopped going to Sunday services, but this relationship involves a deep regard and affection for one of its schools of theology: Meadville Lombard Theological School.

Without being able to articulate it, I think this is what I was looking for during the end of my time in New York and what I'd began to uncover in my feelings toward that Roxbury playground and what it signified for me. In that bit of concrete and steel in the inner city of Boston, life involved a type of desperation that the church couldn't address through its bag of theological and ritual tricks; humanism gave me a way to replace that desperation through an acquaintance with the rhythms and the geography of human life in its varied and vibrant forms.

The desire to structure life and to find importance in what we think and do isn't a process owned by those who believe in God unless we, humanists, foolishly give up that component of meaning-making.

I understand that some of the ways in which this process has been worked out—such as gods, angels, demons, Santa Claus, and so on—are of no substance. We don't do ourselves any good kowtowing to the superstitions of theists, but maintaining a hard line regarding their fantasies shouldn't mean surrendering to theists every bit of vocabulary that speaks to the awe of life. Ritual—or even religion—doesn't have to be a bad word if we don't assume that what theists say about it is all that can be said about it, and that the way they describe ritual is the only way ritual can be described. My journey from evangelical Christianity to humanism taught me this much.

My journey isn't unlike that of others, and this convinces me that life for humanists and atheists requires opportunities for reflecting on our relationships, the signs and symbols that map out our godless worldview. This doesn't mean we are turning to supernatural mumbo jumbo or falling back into superstition. Ritual can be as simple as gathering on a given day of the week to talk about shared interests and concerns or regularly getting together to do community service. Something about human life—the realization that we labor in this world without cosmic oversight—requires regular reflection and thoughtful acknowledgment. My life outside the church involved a growing appreciation for this bit of truth, but there were few times when I could think about this or talk about it without the issue of race also popping up.

I've not been shy over the years about expressing my frustration and my suggestions for changing the way we Unitarian Universalists do things. What I have to say about this is typically an extension of my response to those well-worn questions: "How do we get more diversity? How do we get more African Americans involved?" Some people ask me that question and quickly follow with a litany of all the anti-racism work they have done, and, in particular, what they and their local congregation have done. My response to that is "If you've been that involved, and have accomplished that much, why are you still asking the same questions asked by congregations less involved in social justice?" Things devolve from there. I should probably avoid that response, but it's what I think . . . so I say it.

Others ask the same question and want more shades of the same answer—different racial and ethnic groups populating the pews—but they don't want these new people to substantively change the way things are done at their church. "Just sit and look exotic" is the implication, or at least that is my takeaway from their comments.

Still another group asks the question, and they actually want to know what to do differently. The question from this third group gives the impression of desperation, a strong sense that things aren't going well and that the health and longevity of the UUA is at stake. These are the people who have a sense of the association's failures and shortcomings, as well as its potential, and they aren't looking for me to pat them on the back and tell them what good work they've done. They aren't blaming racial minorities for not finding them and their churches appealing. They don't want a foolproof plan and aren't looking for me to do all the work for them; they just want some sense of where to start. And while this approach is the preferable one, it still presents a problem: Why would I, one individual African American humanist, have the answer when it comes to attracting all other African Americans? I have some suggestions, but I can't provide the detailed blueprint. This situation is a throwback to the "special status" I encountered when I was a young preacher: that the minister had knowledge beyond that of others. But for this group of people, my stature wasn't the result of some type of cosmic anointing; it was the consequence of the superficial markers of race on/in my body. The social construct of race was the new calling, the new source of authority, and members of the UUA wanted to tap into it.

Chapter Fifteen

DON'T MESS WITH TEXAS

Macalester College was a good place for me. It's where I learned to teach, develop my research agenda, experience the politics of academic life, and where I took my humanism public. Even so, there was something missing.

It was my goal to eventually combine undergraduate education with the mentoring of graduate students. In Minnesota there were no options for me, no PhD programs in the study of religion in which I could craft a concentration in the study of African American religion. I'd have to leave Macalester and Minnesota in order to have graduate students. I lived every dimension of my life with departure in mind, even as my private life became more complex.

I married during my time at Macalester. In hindsight, Cheryl Johnson, the gossip columnist for the Minneapolis *StarTribune*, might not have appreciated the matter-of-fact way in which I made it clear very early in our relationship that Minnesota wasn't home for me. But I thought I needed to put my cards on the table, say what I thought, and let the relationship thrive or die with that honesty. It went something like this: "I can't finish out my career here. I want to someday work with graduate students. I understand that you have your job here, but you should know what I'm planning . . . if this thing is going to get serious." She seemed to understand and went along with the plan, as far as I could discern, at least in theory.

I didn't have a particular place in mind. The academy doesn't necessarily work that way. There was a range of schools I thought might be a good fit, should they have openings at some point. But I didn't think in terms of,

"Well, it's this region, or this school, or nothing." There were places I never imagined myself living, just because they were so foreign to me, but I like to believe I was always open to a range of possibilities. I'd never been the type of academic who thought of stature in my field of study as tied to a particular school. I believed my standing was based on the work I accomplished wherever I was teaching.

When I received a call from Rice University in Houston, Texas, it was nothing I'd anticipated. I was familiar with Rice because I'd applied there when I first entered the job market. I got offers from Macalester and Bowdoin before Rice determined the second round of interviews. And there was no way I would surrender a job for the prospect of an interview, so I contacted the chair of the search and told him that I was withdrawing from consideration. The school didn't cross my mind after that point. I was too absorbed with trying to make my way at Macalester.

Years later I received a call asking if I'd consider coming to Rice for a semester as a Lynette Autry Visiting Professor. After a couple of conversations with Rice, with my wife and my mentor, Calvin Roetzel, I decided to accept the invitation.

I'd never spent any time in the Deep South, nor had I ever imagined myself living there. Everything I knew about Texas, sadly, was gathered for the most part from songs and television shows like *Dallas*. So, stereotypes about Texans shaped much of what I thought I understood about the state—big hair, cowboy boots, ten-gallon (whatever that meant) hats, Wrangler jeans, thick accents, and loads of money made off oil and cattle. I'd only been to Houston once before, and that was during July, when I traveled with Richard Ammons to meet with Macalester graduates. I remember thinking to myself as the hot, humid day smacked me in the face, "Damn. How do people deal with this? If there could be a hell, it would have to feel like this."

Old wisdom indicates it isn't a good idea to rule things out, so "Never say never." This came home to me, and despite my previous strong feelings, I arrived at the Houston airport with my roller bag, briefcase, and another small bag ready for a semester at Rice University. I brought a few suits with me for work. My choice of suits over more casual attire in the Houston heat threw a lot of people who assumed I didn't know better, but as the semester went on, they realized it wasn't a mistake on my part. I meant to wear suits, the Houston heat be damned! What they found more odd, however, was my choice of an apartment—something modest and inconsistent with the wealth of Rice and the social standing of its faculty.

The apartment was small, but it was sufficient for what I needed. Even the pounding rain on the window air-conditioning unit—the bang of water against the metal—was easy enough to overlook. Monday through Friday I'd walk or catch the bus to campus and then walk or catch the bus back to my apartment. For much of my time in Houston I didn't have a television—unusual, because I normally watch a lot of television—so I'd read and listen to the radio. There was something about this more austere lifestyle that I found appealing. I enjoyed the time away from some of the least appealing aspects of my life in Minnesota and found that it better fit my introvert tendencies. There were no functions to attend with my wife, no small talk, no large expectations on campus for visiting faculty—just time to do my work without interruption, Monday through Friday.

Sundays were a blur, but every Saturday began with a call to my mother as I ran my errands in Houston. Periodically she'd ask, "Where are we now?" And I'd respond, maybe with a location: "Ma, we're walking to the grocery store." We'd always been close, but I've never liked talking on the phone. In Houston this changed; we communicated—shared bright spots in our week, discussed challenges. I'd catch up on her activities and family developments, and I'd tell her about my work at Rice and about life in Houston.

I didn't know a great deal about Rice beyond its reputation. The undergraduates at Rice and Macalester were similar in terms of intellectual abilities, but there were also some clear distinctions. The Rice students were much more respectful of authority and less willing to push boundaries. I remember during my first class, I introduced myself and told them I was from Macalester College. After the class, as I was leaving, I overheard one of the students say something like "I have a friend at Macalester College," and with a bit of shock in her voice, she said, "Can you believe they call their professors by their first names!" Those to whom she said this shared her surprise. It wasn't something that was going to happen at Rice.

There was a clear difference in terms of recognized authority, and, while students loaded up on majors and minors, my initial experience of Rice under-graduates was high accountability and responsibility. At the start of one of my classes, a student said most of them hadn't finished the reading; they apologized for that and asked if I would be willing to join them for dinner or lunch later in the week and we could use that as a time to catch up on the class discussion. My students at Macalester were great and the school is wonderful, but I don't recall ever having that type of exchange there. I heard plenty of "There is too much work. We have other classes,"—yes, but never "My bad, I didn't finish my work and I apologize for wasting your time, Professor Pinn." I can't say this was the general ethos at Macalester, but it was part of my experience.

Working with the undergraduates was a good experience, but what really got me up in the morning and walking through that Houston heat was conversation with some of my colleagues and graduate students. Things were going well, and I was enjoying being there. From the very start, it all seemed good to me, but I didn't have a sense of what people at Rice thought about me being there.

Shortly after my first month on campus, I was called to the dean's office late one afternoon. I'd started exercising in attempt to get in shape, drop a few pounds, and avoid some of the health concerns men of my age in my family tend to develop. I was just back in my office, covered in sweat after working out when the phone rang. "The dean would like to see you." I didn't know what this was about. Had I offended? Had I broken some Rice code I didn't know about? "I'm just back from the gym. I'd like to shower first. I don't want to come to Gale's office covered in sweat," was something along the lines of my reply. The response threw me a bit. I expected his assistant to say, "Sure no problem. Can we say twenty minutes?" But no, the response was for me to come right away, no need to shower first.

I dried my face, walked down the two flights of stairs, and was quickly led to his office. Gale Stokes smiled and motioned for me to take a seat. I said, "I'm just back from the gym and I don't want to get sweat all over your furniture." His response, with that smile still on his face, was something like, "Don't be silly, have a seat." I sat, and before I could get comfortable—knowing I was leaving a sweat print that would be apparent as soon as I got up again—he began to speak.

Gale told me that the Religious Studies Department had met and requested he offer me a permanent appointment. He said he was prepared to offer me an endowed chair because I deserved it and compensation commensurate with the position. I assumed at that point he would tell me a contract would be written up and I'd be given some time to review it. But instead he asked what it would take to get me to Rice. What would it take to get me to rich and highly ranked Rice University? I had no clue how to answer that question, but I'd learned enough in earlier negotiations—including job offers while at Macalester—to know I shouldn't even try at that point.

Gale said there was no rush, but Rice would want a response as quickly as I could provide. We shook hands, and I got up from the couch hoping he wouldn't see the sweat stain and, if he did, that it wouldn't leave a bad impression.

Although this was never mentioned, I knew that if I accepted the offer I would become the first African American full professor to hold an endowed chair at the university. I would be in a much larger department at a tier-one research university, and I would have the freedom to develop a PhD concentration in the study of African American religion. There was already at least one person interested in applying for admissions in order to work with me, and the possibilities for creating something great at Rice seemed without limit. Yet the negative reaction to my humanism stance in Minnesota was still on my mind, and I wondered how it would play out in what I understood as rather evangelical and conservative Texas. I didn't want to meet the same hostility again, especially in a place not even marketed as "nice."

It could be a good place for me, but there were issues to address. I started making phone calls. My mentor at Macalester College, Calvin Roetzel, said he knew this day was coming but that he was grateful for what I'd given to Macalester. He said little to try to dissuade me, although some other colleagues made attempts. My mother was delighted and so proud. Maybe she thought the Bible Belt and its intense commitment to Christianity packed just the wallop I needed to get me back on the path of faith.

The conversation with my wife needed to take place in person, although I called to tell her there were some professional possibilities we needed to discuss. I left for Minneapolis that Thursday, as I did every other weekend, and we talked. My wife, who was typically expressive, was guarded. So I kept pressing to make certain we were on the same page. We both knew this day would come; we'd talked about it. But now it wasn't a theory; it was a reality. No longer was it just a vague plan; it was a matter of packing up, moving, and leaving behind all that was familiar. The decision couldn't be rushed. If I took the job, I didn't want her to resent me. If I didn't and stayed at Macalester, would I resent her? Would this be my best—and last—opportunity to take that next step in my professional life? This situation would have been hard enough without a commute, but trying to do this while I was in Houston most of the time and she was in Minneapolis led to a different level of stress.

Gale was generous with time, but when the offer made in early February was still without a response in April, he started to get a bit nervous. He'd stop by my office to check in, and I'd tell him that such a major decision required time and that I needed to make certain it was right for my family. He understood but finally gave me a deadline. And it wasn't until the afternoon on that last day—sometime in May—that I walked the signed contract into his office. I was leaving Macalester and moving to Rice, but only after my wife said I should take the job and she'd figure out her situation.

I didn't resign my position at Macalester immediately because I'd promised one of my colleagues I would chair her tenure committee and I had to be tenured faculty at Macalester in order to do that. However, I knew being there beyond that fall semester would be tough, so I agreed to be a visiting faculty member at Williams College.

That fall semester everyone knew I was leaving, and it made things a bit awkward. My closest friends and I would remain in contact, that much was for certain, but it meant thinking about a different way of communicating with them without the benefit of a short car ride or opportunities to hang out after work.

I was transitioning away from Macalester and preparing for some months in Williamstown, where I'd teach one course and give a series of lectures. Away from everything familiar, I'd also have uninterrupted time for writing, when I wasn't traveling to the Albany airport heading to Minnesota.

I'd thought things were in place with my wife, but the tension and reluctance on her part to really engage in a new life in Houston should have told me something about our situation. Although, for someone making a living by communicating information, she might have been more communicative with me about this huge change in our life circumstances. The distance served to expose what were deep and persistent problems. I went along with counseling as a way to address the problems, although the time away felt better and more comforting than it should have for a married man. It entailed months of alone time, with only my work occupying me.

I felt an odd sense of relief when I finally packed up some of the furniture, some of my clothing, and a few other items and headed to Houston.

I'd only been at Rice a short time, and while my professional life was advancing, my personal life was not. My marriage was falling apart and my mother passed away. Although I'd been prepared for my mother's death at a young age due to her ongoing health concerns, a stabilizing force in my life was gone. Her death in 2005 left quite a large hole, but I always knew she loved me and was proud of me, and I loved her. My mother's passing brought my siblings and me closer together, but it also meant the link between me and my extended family was gone.

Friends and colleagues reached out to me during this time, but none with more force, persistence, and welcoming arms than Juan and Stacey Floyd-Thomas. We'd known each other for a few years, but with my mother's passing, they, along with Janet Floyd, "Mother" Floyd, and Mrs. Thomas, welcomed me into their family. They are committed Christians and I am a humanist, but our interactions show—to the extent this is possible—the capacity of dissimilar people to bracket particular differences on philosophy and ideologies for the sake of a shared commitment to the integrity of life. We have heated debates and conversations that, for the uninitiated who don't understand our relationship, come across as something close to knockdown, drag-out fights. On occasion I accompany them to church with the hope that they'll come to recognize their theism could be appreciated for its cultural value—its contributions to cultural production—without needing to embrace its supernatural claims. Church is a spiritual experience for them, connecting them to the divine; for me, it was like going to a museum or some other cultural activity. I'd try to do with their rituals what the great humanist literary figure James Weldon Johnson did with the African American tradition of the sermon in *God's Trombones*. He didn't write this depiction of the sermonic style of African Americans because he believed in the truth of the Christian faith's claims; he did so because the sermonic style marked a dimension of African American culture. Going to church with these friends was nothing but a cultural activity for me. Church is an element of culture without special truths. It was possible to love theists—Juan and Stacey and their families—without buying their fantasies and illusions about spiritual forces.

Friends at Rice also helped with this personal and professional transition. Outside the Religious Studies Department (particularly Elias Bongmba, Jeffrey Kripal, and William Parsons), there were Alex Byrd, Ed Cox, and Caroline Levander.

I first encountered Alex over the phone when I invited him to participate in the small conference I was cosponsoring on the campus while I was a visiting faculty member. He agreed to it, and we had an opportunity to talk during that weekend, and we hit it off immediately. I met Ed during my semester at Rice, and his advice and wise counsel helped on so many levels. Both Alex and Ed became my allies, sounding boards, and friends. We don't get together as often as we'd like, but the connection remains strong—and this is important on a campus with a limited African American presence.

People mentioned Caroline Levander to me when I was a visiting faculty member. Alex and others would say, "You need to meet Caroline." However, I didn't meet her during that semester. I met Caroline when she and Alex contacted me at Williams to ask if I'd be interested in participating in a new venture they were developing called the Americas Colloquium. I, of course, agreed, and once I arrived on campus, it didn't take long for us to become great friends—we enjoyed talks over coffee, the occasional dinner, movies, and plays. We connected, and I'm grateful. She introduced me to distance running and Houston's cultural outlets, and our shared interest in the intellectual nature and meaning of boundaries and borders meant conversations concerning the academic challenges posed by notions of the nation/state. These conversations gave me a way to expand my sense of the nature and meaning of African American religion, defined as it is in significant ways by the symbol and reality of movement.

My personal life centering on Minneapolis was coming to an end—

although for two years I continued to commute back and forth—and Caroline, Alex, and Ed became important parts of a new life in Houston. And this bit of relief undergirded advances in my professional life as my personal life changed in a significant way. My wife and I finally filed for divorce, and I began to spend time moving between Houston and Minneapolis dealing with my attorney, her attorney and the judge, dividing up belongings and closing that chapter of my life.

My work at Rice was an opportunity to give humanism more robust academic attention from the perspective of cultural studies and religious studies. Both God and godlessness were important to me but in very different ways. God was important as an idea that still dominated so much of African American thought and practice, and I wanted to understand what this entailed. But godlessness was important to me for personal reasons—it is my life stance—and for professional reasons in that it is an underappreciated dimension of African American life in particular and of life in general in the United States. While many of my colleagues involved in the study of African American religion find it a bit more difficult to accept, I found this resistance and at times hostility toward my posture more amusing than upsetting. I think of my work as wrestling over ideas; it isn't personal for me. I can disagree over and dislike the ideas presented by a colleague without that devolving into personal dislike and hard feelings.

I felt a need to push beyond apologetics for humanism to a more robust outlining of it. And I wanted and needed to do this in a way that broke the grip of theists on my discipline of theology. Even though I'd given up on notions of God and all the accompanying trappings of theism, I wouldn't give up on theology as an intellectual tool. My life had involved paradox and tensions for as long as I could remember, and I had no reason to believe this would end with my conversion to godlessness. I was a theologian, by training and inclination, who didn't believe in God. I certainly wasn't the first to hold this position, but that historical record did little to make the tension easier for my colleagues to understand.

I spent a good deal of time trying to map out the look of the new PhD program in African American religion at Rice. While I still planned to teach undergraduate courses, I'd also have responsibility for training/mentoring graduate students in a way that would allow them to make important con-tributions to the study of religion. For some, there are moral implications regarding the preparation of graduate students for the job market: since there is no guarantee of a job, some feel it is not morally or ethically sound to par-ticipate in students' training. I couldn't promise students jobs, but I could promise to provide them with the best training I could offer.

My students work from the basic premise that religion involves a way of naming and structuring human experience. It isn't a unique form of experi-ence but rather involves a way of thinking about and categorizing efforts to make life meaningful. They share with me this thinking, but I don't believe in cloning myself through my students. I've not been concerned with producing generations that develop projects identical to what I produce. From my per-spective, that's too boring a way to think about my contribution to advanced training. If the students are doing good work, it should extend well beyond what I do. They should be wrestling with questions and ideas that extend well beyond what I would have imagined. At its best, the work of my students should push me to think of new ideas, to read and study, to expand my cat-egories, and to enhance my teaching. Maybe some would become humanists or would write about humanism; but even if they didn't, they would teach and research in a way that was open to a more expansive sense of the religious world and its tools. They wouldn't be thrown by the idea of a humanist reli-gion without god or a theology that is completely godless, nor would they be thrown by claims to secular existence.

If I'm doing it right, teaching graduate students in this way will keep me on my intellectual and professional toes for a long time. However, I couldn't avoid the contradiction that was staring me in the face. I was committed to humanism and understood it as having both personal and professional impor-tance, but I wasn't willing to admit students into the PhD program at Rice who believed the same thing and wanted to explore humanism as part of their training. It wasn't simply a matter of telling them to wait until they had tenure to do that sort of controversial work, not when I'd first published on the topic while still a junior member of the Macalester faculty. Maybe some of it was a—perhaps unconscious—desire to protect them from some of the negative responses I'd encountered? I'm not certain if that's the case. I do, however, know there are very few positions available on the job market for a career explicitly in humanism, despite a growing number of secular studies programs at colleges and universities. So, I need to mentor and train students consistent with their interests, Rice resources (intellectual and financial), and in line with what the job market demands. Students receiving a PhD from Rice under my direction have a more flexible sense of the religious world than most, and so they are open to the importance, the value, and the continual presence of atheism and humanism inside and outside their area of study.

Unlike some of my colleagues, I have no plans to retire—why give up the job just when I've started to figure it out? So I continue this work I began at Rice, looking forward to a good number of years of activity, marked by undergraduates who expand their critical thinking skills and by graduate students who make important and lasting contributions to the profession. Some might label what I do as a particular calling or vocation. Maybe, but I see it simply as a basic obligation to a life I love. I didn't present myself in a particular way for the glory of God; it was about honoring myself and representing my communities well.

There's something about this stance that made me feel like an intellectual "badass," complete with a suit (my favorite thing to wear), a small diamond stud in my left ear, stylish glasses, bald head, shining shoes, and an animated style of speaking that developed when I started preaching. I'd lost my belief in God, but something about the style of conversation and vocation stayed with me. I'd always been a fan of dress clothes, and being godless didn't mean I had to rethink my personal aesthetic.

I was a professional academic, a theologian with some standing, and I wanted to present humanism as a new mode of theological inquiry that dismantled the idea that theology had to have a god or gods at its base. I'd joined the procession of thinkers who worked to free theology from supernaturalism and expose it as a method for getting a sense of how humans talk about human experience in an effort to come to grips with the issues and concerns that matter most to human life. And I'd do this work in connection with good friends and colleagues like Katie Cannon and Peter Paris, who've mentored me in the profession and pushed me for greater clarity regarding the alternative I want to provide. I owe them much: gratitude and good work worthy of the conversations and exchanges we've had over the years.

Theism produces sloppy ways of thinking because it doesn't necessarily respect reason but instead favors fiction. At least this was my experience of it, and as a minister I'd contributed to this problem. As an academic, I'd make amends for this.

Chapter Sixteen

WHOSE HUMANISM?

I have no plans to give up my right to voice my opinion, to critique both theists and the godless. There's too much enjoyment in the process, and I value the exchanges too much to surrender it for the sake of some type of "cease-fire." I speak my mind.

My stance has been years in the making and has involved a move away from the comforts of my childhood. I don't miss those comforts; some people find this hard to believe, but it's true. How or why would I miss illusions, things made up, when they'd been replaced with a much firmer grasp on reality?

As a theist I'd struggled to appear good enough and to say and do something that would point in the direction of a larger reality, some sort of cosmic force working behind the scenes of my life. As a godless humanist, just being a good person, aware and appreciative of life—with a desire to make the conditions of and for life healthier—is good enough.

I don't miss God. I also don't spend a great deal of time beating myself up for having believed in God. No "What ifs" or "How could I have been so stupid?" internal conversations. There's no need to second-guess myself—nothing to be gained through those mental gymnastics. I never wondered if I would move back to the church begging for forgiveness and serving as the poster child for God's grace and love, and the foolishness of human self-importance. While that would make quite a story, complete with media attention, letters and cards from supporters, and speaking engagements, there was no way it was going to happen. No.

I encountered so many people with differing philosophies and viewpoints claiming the label that it was difficult to determine if humanism had a stable definition that cut across regions, groups, and politics. Were any distinctions I might bring up in my work and in my conversations just background noise? My sense of what humanism should accomplish was straightforward, but what humanism actually entails was a much more complicated thing. It is a way of thinking about life and a way of living life, a system of ethics and a moral code. But in light of these many possibilities, who is a humanist? And because one is godless, is one an atheist or a humanist, or both? Or, maybe neither label works well?

There is something about humanism and atheism that is deeply subjective and that requires tools of analysis that recognize the manner in which both involve a certain type of belief, not supernatural and not based in superstition, but belief. I'd come to recognize that the godless assumption that activism can make a difference, despite the fickle nature of humans, is a matter not of certainty but of belief—a material-based hope. While some uncertainty is always present in even the best of our circumstances, a willingness on the part of godless people to work in spite of this paradox isn't captured by the scientific method and isn't necessarily premised on anything solidly objective and without emotion.

From college on, I'd come to understand the importance of the scientific method; it was part of the core conversation for academic inquiry as we were learning to understand it in higher education. So, I had an appreciation for the sciences and understood my work as a theologian to involve an approach just as committed to rigor and verifiability. But I had a deep regard for ethics, for proper movement through the world. This deep regard for being good as a guide for doing good, as Henry David Thoreau would put it, had nothing to do with what God wanted; instead I was concerned with what humans ought to do to forge what is necessary to foster a healthy world.

Much of what I learned to dislike—no, really to despise—about theism involved the fact that it isn't organic. It isn't drawn from the experiences of the people, isn't consistent with the material nature of life. It's poorly fitted to its new purpose, kind of like trying to force a square peg into a round hole. It can be done, but at what cost?

What I mean to say is, theism, at least as I experienced it over the course of my life in the form of Christianity, is a borrowed story—from the beginning of the ridiculous and confused narrative of creation in the Bible through the Book of Revelation. Christianity, I grew to see, is a form of voyeurism supplemented through fantasy enactments and disassociation. My time in Boston, at Grant Church, across from the playground, demonstrated that theistic faith requires a type of schizophrenia: life in a spiritual world versus life in a material world. It promotes a spiritual version of life, free from the responsibilities and sense of accountability that accompany maturity.

No burning bushes, no booming voices from on high, no miracles, and no special revelations given to servants that have been picked miraculously by God. I was content. I knew better than to be too optimistic and too certain, but I was as content with my godless take on life as I could be. There were always frustrations and problems, but these things weren't shaking my fundamental commitment to my godless movement through the world.

My love of the blues and my deep regard for the writer Richard Wright have helped me with this posture toward the world. Neither Wright nor the blues provide easy answers that draw humans away from the world and from themselves, but they motivate me all the same.

I've listened to the blues for a long time, but I don't recall this interest in the blues stemming from hearing the music in my home as a child. We had a family stereo in the living room, and while I had my own little player, I loved using that stereo and going through the albums that belonged to my family. They were varied and a bit mysterious to me as a child. There was Redd Foxx and other raw comics, Freddie Fender, the gospel greats, yes, but the blues—no.

From the cassettes I played to the CDs I now own, I am enraptured by the earthiness, the playfulness, and the appreciation for embodied life exemplified in the blues lyrics. I don't simply mean the blues as defined by the "race records" of the early twentieth century. I mean going further back to the blues that existed in the rough terrain of slave plantations and crop fields and that held its own against the theistic ranting of the spirituals. Blues going back those many centuries championed a life not marked by superstition and hope based on cosmic fantasies, and motivated listeners to appreciate the ordinary and mundane elements of life, those dimensions of human experience not favored in churches.

Having been in the pulpit, I am convinced theists within African American communities often despised the blues and labeled blues tunes "devil music" out of a fear of truth—a concern that if people thought about their conditions and circumstances in the way the blues encouraged, they might turn their questioning to black churches. All the things churches tried to ignore, hide, or punish—the things I'd once preached against—were discussed differently within the blues. The pleasures and joys the body can give and receive that are uncomfortable within church circles are sought and celebrated within the blues.

Blues figures and church figures both encountered injustices and adverse circumstances, but, while church figures seek assistance from God or find a way to make their predicament a source of inspiration and even joy, blues figures "keep on keeping on." The blues sees nothing special, no cosmic plan expressed in human misery. It's just the shit we encounter and that we have to move through. There is a sense of vulnerability in the blues, a celebration of paradox and tension that better explains the things that confronted me at that Roxbury playground.

If the blues took the form of prose, and just prose, those tunes would tell a story similar to those told by Richard Wright. I first encountered his books as a college student, and even then there was something both compelling and troubling about the world he painted. It was a world of misery with only glimmers of hope easily crushed by the weight of racial discrimination externalized and internalized by African Americans. The absurdity of life, the existential traumas of human existence carried Wright and his characters from the South to the North without much change in circumstances.

When I first encountered him as a college student, and as a Christian, I wanted to address from within the church the injustices he outlined. I believed the Christian Church, properly constituted and activated, could wipe out the frustrations and limitations on life experienced by his characters. As a Christian, I appreciated Wright's critique of society and wanted to do something to prove his challenge to theism misguided.

I continued to read him as a graduate student and endorsed his social critique while becoming more open to his view of theism. My social gospel could absorb his social critique, but it couldn't manage his critique of theism as a force that paralyzes our will and contaminates our thinking processes. I wrestled with Wright over his rejections of my faith and his depiction of women as faithful servants duped into belittling themselves for the sake of some made-up God figure. What he saw in Christian women wasn't what I wanted to see in my mother and the other women I knew who gave themselves to the service of the church. And while I could find some usefulness in the church, the playground across the street from Grant Church gave Wright's argument the edge. So much of what he described about Chicago decades before I arrived in Boston were echoed in the limited options and the decay represented for me by that playground.

I still believe there are dimensions of Wright's vision of life that are problematic and can't be fully accepted. Yet his godlessness and his comfort with being so, as well as the language he uses to describe that stance, are things from which I draw. It is not a direct correlation between his take on godlessness and my understanding of humanism, but his realism has offered me food for thought over the years.

His work is on my mind regularly, and when I walk in cities where he once lived I look for the spots that impacted him, and I think about what it must have been like to be an African American atheist living in Chicago or Paris. And I wonder what he would have thought about more recent developments within humanism and atheism in general, and African American involvement with godless organizations in particular. Would he be suspicious of what these organizations offer? Is there some version of "What would Wright do?" that African Americans ought to invoke on occasion, or that at least I should, as an admirer of his writings?

Wright and blues share a type of swagger, a posture toward the world that is bold, creative, and organic. I like to believe the way of being that they express has been more recently captured in the hip-hop culture. Mind you, I've never had "skills"—could never rap, didn't have the abilities of the graffiti artist, couldn't dance in the gravity-defying manner of the breakers, and could only adopt the more conservative elements of the hip-hop style: the haircuts, the Africa pendant, and maybe a shirt or two. But embracing the culture of hip-hop was within my reach.

I have thought for a long time now that cultural sources like the blues, literature, and hip-hop offer humanist and atheist communities important challenges and tools. And, any opportunity I get, I talk about and share this as much as possible. These cultural forms speak to me in large part because I see myself reflected in them. My sense of life and its meaning echoes what blues artists, humanist writers, and hip-hop's earthy sensitivities paint as the world.

As with my preaching years ago, I continue to hold to the opinion that we can only make information available, and people will do what they will with it. The difference is that back then I believed in a God who gave me an edge by convicting sinners and bringing backsliders to Christ. Now, people come or not for much more mundane reasons. With my preaching, divine forces intervened, but as a godless lecturer and researcher, I understand something as simple as laundry, a television program, an ill child, or a grocery list can keep people from my talks. There is no divine mystery in that absence; it is just a matter of getting all the chores done in the limited time people have to themselves. The demands of ordinary life take priority.

Chapter Seventeen

STAKING A CLAIM

While I spent time and energy trying to carve out a space in which to be a humanist and do humanism, my particular humanist way of thinking and doing had to be about more than fighting theists. Any other approach gave theists too much power, made them godlike. And the way we position them and discuss their influence gives them a trans-historical reality, a kind of superhuman presence.

The establishment of a reasonable world marked by theism limited to the private realm of life would work for me, but so many atheists talk about and celebrate the end of religion—but they keep the theists around as the super-embodiment of the religion they detest. If nothing else, "religious people" become an omnipresent "straw man" debated and verbally slapped around at banquets, conferences, meetings, and more casual social gatherings. Theism is ever present, a shadow figure lurking in thoughts and informing the actions of many godless people.

This game doesn't require a great deal of information. Anecdotes work just fine. Is mockery enough? It is as if there is merit—a badge of courage and bravery—in castigating religion. After all, why spend time learning anything about what can't be confirmed through scientific investigation? Why learn anything about this cultural material called religion that has shaped so much of human history?

I know firsthand the harm religion can do, but I also appreciate the people who are using it to try to make their way through life; and while I reject their beliefs, I have to respect them as persons, and this means approaching them with high regard for their humanity, despite how underdeveloped their will and insights might be. I think this is not only a pragmatic approach, but it is also a responsible and ethically mature response to the tangled web of life and the need for activity that respects shared humanity while acknowledging our differences.

Simply telling me about the evils of theism is insufficient. I already know. That's why I left the church. Simply reiterating the point is overkill and does little, as far as I can tell, to bring people in. That is not to say some don't come into godless organizations as a result of this approach; they do. But not with the type of numbers these organizations need and want.

I understand, and I have embraced the need to critique and push against theism. Such critiques should be done, however, based on more than anecdotes. They should be grounded in the same intellectual rigor that informs our approach to scientific knowledge. And I'd come to believe deconstruction of theism had to be followed by a constructive and affirming process of services, of ritual structures for joys and sorrows, and all the other structures for meaningful life within the contemporary world. This, I was growing to believe, had to also involve partnerships.

This might involve work with some of the very Christians I thought I'd left behind. How exactly to do this is something I'll have to work out, and I'll have to do so being mindful of my growing reluctance to "join." I tend to be suspicious of groups, aware of how group mentality and behavior can be counterproductive. However, it's not an extreme reluctance on my part. Perhaps this godless recognition of community, of relationships as fundamental, is a dimension of the Unitarian Universalism in me? Perhaps, despite elements of my critique, something of the Unitarian Universalist warm feelings toward gatherings persist in me on some level and in some way; perhaps the glow from the flame of the chalice is present somewhere within me?

I knew I'd have to push myself beyond my comfort zone, deal with my introvert tendencies, and work with organizations and groups by attending meetings, giving talks to humanists and atheists, and encouraging collaboration.

I must admit that I went into my godless life with a wrongheaded assumption that things within the humanist and atheist organizations would be different. Although I didn't come out and say it, I still had a small assumption that oppressed and marginalized godless people would be very sensitive to injustice and would be less likely to perpetuate it within their ranks. I knew this wasn't the case in the same way experiencing racism doesn't keep African Americans from being sexist or experiencing homophobia doesn't prevent gays and lesbians from being classist or racist.

The godless have a different perspective on the nature and meaning of life in the world, but they were born into and taught with the same social norms as the theists. The sense of who people are and the significance of superficial differences of skin tone, hair texture, gender, and so on is learned early, long before most people make a public pronouncement of their disbelief or belief. Our social conditioning is very similar regardless of what we say about God or gods.

Still, I've encountered humanists and atheists who seem to believe being godless and committed to science and reason is a prophylactic against injustice and irrational discrimination. They argue that ethics is a fundamental component of science and that horrific events like the Tuskegee Experiment weren't science. They smile and say this to me . . . to a black male whose relationship to medicine isn't completely divorced from scientific racism? This is a bad move, not the way to go for organizations that want to tap into the growing number of African Americans who do not affiliate with any particular religious (theistic) community.

Even when African Americans find places where they are with likeminded others, they are never too far away from a potential bad reaction to their decision: the loss of family and friends or marginalization within atheist and humanist organizations. There is no space for African American atheists and humanists that doesn't hold the threat of a negative statement about race or gender, and I would imagine this is also the case for Hispanics and other minority groups as well. And organizations have taken note.

At the large conferences and conventions, the buzz about embracing difference is thick and at times rather loud. There isn't a blanket response to issues of diversity and the proper role of social justice issues in the thinking and doing of the godless.

I've come a long way—from evangelical Christian to proud humanist without God. The journey has had its twists and turns and its rough patches.

Still, I've never doubted my departure from the church. I've never looked back because I've never had reason to look back.

I maintain a somewhat suspicious attitude toward life. Many people think I'm pessimistic, but I prefer to say that I operate out of a keen sense of realism. Preparing for the worst and being pleasantly surprised if it doesn't happen, but ready if it does, has remained my posture toward the world. I think, despite the opinions of others, it has served me well.

When I believed in and trusted in God as the final authority regarding my life, this suspicious attitude was still in place because I had a sense of people as born into evil through original sin; now I maintain this suspicion out of a solid recognition of just how fragile human ethics and morality can be. Even people with the best of intentions can do you harm, and there's no God or gods in place to look out for you when people do you wrong.

So I say, be prepared, be ready, even when you're smiling and shaking hands. I am not a prince, but even in my world, bits and pieces of Niccolò Machiavelli's thought (for example, be mindful of the political ramifications of words and deeds, and push for respect)—as well as the wisdom of Richard Wright, playwright Lorraine Hansberry, and other godless figures who acknowledge human frailty and human potential—seem to be relevant: different times, different circumstances, but still dealing with people.

I don't think of myself as cold-blooded and calculating—others have their own opinions about that—but over the years I have remained cautious, and I assess situations so as to be able to leave them with my integrity and well-being as intact as possible.

I left the church in order to be true to the hard questions pressing on me, to affirm life, to celebrate and mourn, to ritualize major moments, all within the fragile arrangements of this world.

I'm on a different path than the one selected by the little preacher in Buffalo. I move through the world without God, yet mindful of my mother's hopes for me embedded in and articulated through my grandmother's remark as she readied herself for me to leave Buffalo: "Move through the world knowing your footsteps matter."

Okay, Ma. Okay, Grandma. Okay . . . I'll keep moving.

READING LIST

What follows is a short list of some of the books that have influenced my thinking over the years. I have partaken in conversations with these authors, some in person, but most took place while I worked through their books at home, in a coffee shop, or on various campuses. It would be a mistake to assume that all those listed below represent writers with whom I agree; to the contrary, I disagree in strong ways with many of them. These books are among those that challenged my thinking and pushed me to ask hard questions because each, in its own way, spoke to human experience and human need. Even those with which I disagree have informed my thinking and helped to shape in some fashion my humanism, my atheism, my perspective on theism and religious organizations.

Baldwin, James. *Go Tell It on the Mountain* (NY: Dial Press Trade, 2000).

Canon, Katie. *Black Womanist Ethics* (Atlanta: Scholars' Press, 1989).

Carson, Clayborne, ed. *The Autobiography of Martin Luther King, Jr.* (NY: Warner Books, 1998).

Cone, James H. *Black Theology & Black Power* (San Francisco: Harper & Row, 1989).

———. *A Black Theology of Liberation*, 2nd ed. (Maryknoll, NY: Orbis Books, 1986).

———. *God of the Oppressed* (NY: Harper & Row, 1975).

———. *Martin & Malcolm & America: A Dream or a Nightmare* (Maryknoll, NY: Orbis Books, 1991).

Davis, Angela. *Women, Race, and Class* (NY: Random House, 1981).

Douglass, Frederick. *Narrative of the Life of Frederick Douglass: An American Slave, Written by Himself* (NY: St. Martin's, 2002).

Du Bois, W. E. B. *Writings* (NY: Library of America, 1987).

Ellison, Ralph. *Invisible Man* (NY: Vintage, 1995).

Fanon, Franz. *Black Skin, White Masks* (1952; NY: Grove Press, 1994).

Foucault, Michel. *Discipline and Punish: The Birth of the Prison* (NY: Vintage Books, 1979).

Franklin, John Hope. *From Slavery to Freedom: A History of Negro Americans*, 5th ed. (NY: Alfred A. Knopf, 1980).

Gilroy, Paul. *The Black Atlantic: Modernity and Double Consciousness* (Cambridge, MA: Harvard University Press, 1993).

Hansberry, Lorraine. *A Raisin in the Sun: A Drama in Three Acts* (NY: Random House, 1959).

Hurston, Zora Neale. *Dust Tracks on a Road* (NY: Harper Perennial Modern Classics, 2010).

———. *Mules and Men* (NY: Harper Perennial, 1990).

———. *Their Eyes Were Watching God* (NY: Harper Perennial Modern Classics, 2006).

Jones, William R. *Is God a White Racist? A Preamble to Black Theology* (Boston: Beacon Press, 1996).

Kaufman, Gordon. *An Essay on Theological Method*, 3rd ed. (NY: Oxford University Press, 2000).

King, Martin Luther, Jr. *Where Do We Go from Here: Chaos or Community?* (Boston: Beacon Press, 1967).

Larsen, Nella. *Quicksand and Passing*, ed. and introduction, Deborah E. McDowell (New Brunswick, NJ: Rutgers University Press, 1986).

Locke, Alain, ed. *The New Negro* (NY: Atheneum, 1986).

Long, Charles H. *Significations* (Philadelphia: Fortress Press, 1986).

Malcolm X. *The Autobiography of Malcolm X* (NY: Penguin Modern Classics, 2001).

Morrison, Toni. *Beloved* (NY: Knopf, 1987).

Paris, Peter J. *The Social Teachings of the Black Churches* (Philadelphia: Fortress Press, 1998).

Raboteau, Albert J. *Slave Religion: The "Invisible Institution" in the Antebellum South* (NY: Oxford University Press, 2004).

Richardson, Marilyn. *Maria W. Stewart, America's First Black Woman Political Writer: Essays and Speeches* (Bloomington: Indiana University Press, 1987).

Thoreau, Henry D. *Walden* (Princeton, NJ: Princeton University Press, 1973).

Thurman, Howard. *The Centering Moment* (Richmond, IN: Friends United Press, 2000).

———. *Deep Is the Hunger* (Richmond, IN: Friends United Press, 2000).

———. *The Inward Journey* (Richmond, IN: Friends United Press, 1971).

———. *The Luminous Darkness: A Personal Interpretation of the Anatomy of Segregation and the Ground of Hope* (NY: Harper & Row, 1965).

Walker, David. *David Walker's Appeal* (1829; Baltimore: Black Classic Press, 1997).

Walker, Alice. *The Color Purple* (NY: Mariner Books, 2003).

———. *Living By the Word: Selected Writings, 1973–1987* (NY: Harcourt Brace Jovanovich, 1988).

Washington, James Melvin, ed. *A Testament of Hope: The Essential Writings of Martin Luther King, Jr.* (San Francisco: Harper & Row, 1986).

Welch, Sharon. *A Feminist Ethic of Risk* (Minneapolis: Fortress Press, 1990).

Wells, Ida B. *Southern Horrors and Other Writings; The Anti-Lynching Campaign of Ida B. Wells, 1892–1900* (NY: St. Martin's Press, 1996).

West, Cornel. *Prophesy Deliverance!* Anniversary ed. (Louisville: Westminster John Knox, 2002).

Williams, Delores S. *Sisters in the Wilderness: The Challenge of Womanist God-Talk* (Maryknoll, NY: Orbis Books, 1993).

Wilmore, Gayraud. *Black Religion and Black Radicalism: An Interpretation of the Religious History of Afro-American People* (Maryknoll, NY: Orbis Books, 1979).

Wright, Richard. *Black Boy (American Hunger)* (NY: Perennial Classics, 1998).

———. *Eight Men* (NY: HarperPerennial, 1996).

———. *Native Son* (NY: Harper & Brothers Publishers, 1940).

———. *The Outsider* (NY: HarperPerennial, 1993).

INDEX OF PEOPLE AND PLACES

INDEX OF SUBJECTS